Problem Children

Problem Children: Special Populations in Delinquency

Robert Hartmann McNamara
and Carrie Coward Bucher

CAROLINA ACADEMIC PRESS
Durham, North Carolina

Library of Congress Cataloging-in-Publication Data
McNamara, Robert Hartmann.
Problem children : special populations in delinquency / Robert
Hartmann McNamara and Carrie Coward Bucher.
 p. cm.
Includes bibliographical references and index.
ISBN 978-1-59460-713-4 (alk. paper)
1. Juvenile delinquency. 2. Problem youth. I. Bucher, Carrie
Coward. II. Title.
HV9069.M4155 2011
364.36--dc23
                             2011035171

Carolina Academic Press
700 Kent Street
Durham, North Carolina 27701
Telephone (919) 489-7486
Fax (919) 493-5668
www.cap-press.com

Printed in the United States of America

To:

*Mary Ann and Dan—the enormity of your gift
continues to amaze and humble me.*
RHM

*I would like to thank all of you who work tirelessly
for the children, and those who are suffering with them,
described in this text.
We are grateful for your efforts.*
CCB

Contents

Tables and Figures

Preface

While the public's concerns about delinquency remain focused on the chronic and violent offender, there are many areas of delinquency that are important and relevant, but do not receive attention in a traditional textbook. This book focuses on a few of those populations, where offenders pose a risk to society, but most of them can be effectively treated. What is needed, of course, is a recognition that such youths are salvageable and that their acts, while offensive and harmful, are a reflection of the trauma they have experienced at some point in their lives. It is a mistake to think of these offenders as destined for a career as an adult criminal since most of the research suggests that treatment is a more appropriate and effective alternative than incarceration or detention. However, the prevailing view of the need to increase the severity of sanctions against juveniles only results in higher rates of recidivism. Thus, while it may be frustrating to think that holding youths accountable for their actions cannot be accomplished through punitive means, it may mean that we have to re-examine the goals and objectives related to youth crime. In other words, in the process of implementing a tough law and order approach to delinquency we may be creating and enhancing the very class of individuals we most fear. Our hope is that this book will shed some light on the nuances and problems relating to behaviors such as juvenile sex offending, prostitution, arson and firestarting, computer hacking, graffiti, underage drinking and smoking as well as gang-related behavior. In short, the public's fears about juvenile crime have overshadowed virtually all aspects of juvenile justice and we appear to be returning to a time when we treated juveniles and adults alike in terms of punishment. There may be good reasons for doing this, however there remain a sizeable portion of youths who are actually victims of neglectful and abusive parents, dysfunctional families, or are caught in difficult circumstances that result in their coming to the attention of the justice process. We believe this book can serve as a starting point for a new dialogue about how to prevent youths from becoming hardened delinquents.

RHM/CCB

Acknowledgments

A project such as this one cannot be undertaken without a significant amount of assistance. As this project was part of a sabbatical, many thanks go to The Citadel Foundation for their financial support. Similarly, we would like to thank Ms. Lesleigh Patton, for her critical editorial eyes, her diligence as a researcher, and her dedication to completing this project. Similarly, Beth Hall of Carolina Academic Press has been a wonderful source of support with this project. Thank you, Beth, for your patience and understanding. No project is possible without the support of family and friends and we extend our heartfelt thanks to our spouses for the time needed to complete our thoughts and transforming them into written chapters.

Problem Children:
Special Populations
in Delinquency

Chapter 1

Introduction

It seems that juvenile delinquency is a topic that gets daily attention in the media. Furthermore, some of the more dramatic instances of crime involving juveniles as offenders are often given considerable attention, creating a perception that this population is prone to violence and lacking in morality, and that the juvenile justice system is simply incapable of effectively punishing or treating them. The public's perception of youths in general and delinquents in particular is a combination of fear and compassion. Some experts point out, for example, that the general public in the United States is fearful of delinquents, particularly gangs and violent offenders.[1] While there may be some element of truth to this perception, in that there are individuals who suffer from a host of pathologies that make any form of treatment or intervention unlikely to be effective, the notion of the teenage population being out of control is unwarranted.

At the same time, however, public opinion polls show that most Americans are still committed to treating juvenile offenders rather than simply punishing them.[2] For instance, according to a 2007 poll sponsored by the National Council on Crime and Delinquency, most Americans favor rehabilitative services for young people, are largely opposed to prosecuting youths in adult courts, and oppose incarcerating youths in adult facilities. The poll also found that:

- 90% of Americans agree that youth crime is a major problem in our communities.
- 66% of respondents believe that decisions to transfer youths to adult court should be made on a case-by-case basis and not be simply a matter of statute or public policy.
- 91% believed that rehabilitative services and treatment for incarcerated youths could help prevent future crimes.

- More than 80% of respondents think that spending on rehabilitative services and treatment for youths will save tax dollars in the long run.
- Approximately 70% of Americans feel that putting youths under age 18 in adult correctional facilities makes them more likely to commit future crimes.
- Nearly 68% of respondents *disagree* that incarcerating youths in adult facilities teaches them a lesson and deters them from committing future crimes.[3]

A number of other polls indicate that politicians and policymakers may have misread the public's concerns about delinquency and offenders. For instance, a report by National Juvenile Justice Network cites several studies about public attitudes towards delinquents that suggest policy changes may have occurred without a careful consideration of the public's actual sentiments towards youths and delinquency. For instance, polls from the Center for Children's Law and Policy, The MacArthur Foundation Research Network on Adolescent Behavior and Juvenile Justice, and the National Council on Crime and Delinquency found that the public:

- Believes rehabilitation and treatment can reduce crime and is willing to pay extra taxes to provide those services.
- Prefers rehabilitation over punishment, even for young people who commit violent crimes.
- Opposes mandatory waiver laws for juveniles who commit felonies at a certain age.
- Believes strongly in a separate juvenile justice system.[4]

In general, these polls, as well as others conducted during the 1990s, when the punitive sentiments towards delinquents were at their peak,[5] suggest that the public is supportive of the treatment philosophy and practices of the juvenile justice system even when it considers youth violence to be a major problem.[6] In other words, citizens do not think the "get-tough" approach is the solution to delinquency.

Other Perceptions of Delinquency

Many policymakers and politicians believe the juvenile justice system has gone "soft" on holding youth accountable for their actions. They believe that teens are not deterred by the potential consequences of the system and *recidivism* (re-arrest rate) is out of control. What we need instead, say many politicians and policymakers, are tougher sanctions for juveniles. Advocates of a "get-tough" approach often point to gang-related violence and the prediction of a "super predator" class of violent youths as the reason behind the increase in juvenile crime.

With regard to the latter, in the 1990s, the leading proponents of the super predator prediction were professors John DiLuilio of Princeton University and James Fox of Northeastern University. Juvenile super predators were described as sociopaths with no moral conscience who were not deterred by the sanctions of the juvenile justice system. Some experts even argued that this new breed of offender had different DNA than their predecessors: these former "crack babies"—the result of substance abuse by their young unmarried mothers while they were pregnant—were genetically predisposed towards violent crime.[7]

Supporters of the super predator argument also concluded that because this cohort of disturbed youths were so violent and irrational, any attempts to change their thinking or behavior were futile. The only reasonable solution was to increase punitive sanctions and to treat these offenders as the violent future adults they would eventually become.[8]

In response to this growing "threat" of juvenile offenders, and the subsequent fear it generated, nearly every state in the early 1990s changed how their justice system responded to violent juveniles. These changes were designed to increase the flow of juveniles into the adult criminal justice system, where the punishments were more severe. For instance, many states adopted legislation that:

- Required juveniles charged with certain violent crimes to be tried as adults.
- Expanded the list of crimes that were excluded from juvenile court jurisdiction.

- Gave prosecutors more discretion to file certain juvenile cases in either juvenile or adult court.
- Broadened the range of offenses for which a juvenile could be tried as an adult.
- Lowered the age at which a juvenile court judge could transfer a youth to adult criminal court.[9]

While the prediction of a super predator cohort of youths failed to materialize, concern about violent juvenile offenders remains high and many of the policies and laws enacted during the 1990s remain in effect.

As we will discuss in future chapters, public policy is often shaped by what is perceived to be the cause of the problem. In the case of violent offenders, the "get-tough" philosophy witnessed in the juvenile justice system comes largely from the perception by officials that these types of individuals make up the bulk of the juvenile offender population.[10]

Fears about delinquents engaging in senseless violence, dissatisfaction with the level of accountability offered by the juvenile justice system, and the belief that youths cannot be rehabilitated has put us at a crossroads with what to do with delinquents. Some experts argue that the United States is getting further and further away from treatment and rehabilitation and more focused on punishment, similar to what is offered in the adult system.[11]

Have we really seen an increase in violence by teens and a willingness to engage in criminal activities or has society taken normal and typical adolescent behavior and recast it in a more negative light? Given that our perceptions are often a function of what we have seen and heard, what role has the media played in shaping our understanding of the nature of crime in general and delinquency in particular?

Media Images of Delinquents

While the media's impact on the study of adult crime has been examined rather extensively, both in terms of the news media as well as Hollywood portrayals of criminals, much less attention has been given to portrayals of delinquents. In fact, very little research has explored media influences on the public's perception of juveniles. One study found that while adult crimes are a significant portion of television news, only about one-third of crime stories involve juveniles, and of those, the vast majority focus on homicide and violent crime.[12] Another study pointed out that the extent and type of juvenile crime, as well as the nature of offenders, is distorted in the news media.[13] Still another study reported that only 1 in 12 local news reports and only 1 in 25 national news stories involved youths, but that nearly half (46%) of these stories involved crime victimization, accidents, or violent juvenile crime. The study also found that the public's perceptions of youths, as often troubled and violent, were less likely to change even if factual information was presented that ran counter to these stereotypes.[14]

What these and other studies suggest is that for most citizens, who have little direct experience with the juvenile justice system, the most available and accessible information on the incidence and nature of juvenile crime comes from television news.[15] If the few stories offered about juveniles involve homicide or other violent crimes, it makes sense that the result is a high level of fear, both of the nature of the problem and about being victimized by juveniles.[16]

What may have occurred is that a few dramatic media accounts have shaped the public's understanding about delinquency, which has generated a higher level of fear than necessary about the extent and severity of juvenile crime in general. This, in turn, has been misinterpreted by policymakers and politicians to mean that citizens want a more punitive answer to the problem.

Social Problems and Youths

In addition to typical developmental issues as well as the cultural challenges surrounding one's generation, there are a number of structural problems that can place youths at risk for engaging in delinquency. These structural factors are beyond the control of the youths or their parents—they are societal level problems that impact the quality of life youths experience as well as influencing the *life chances* or opportunities they may obtain. Examples include poverty, the increased costs of housing and transportation, a changing labor market, and inadequate educational opportunities in some school districts.

Risk and Protective Factors

In addition to responding to structural problems like poverty, unemployment, housing, and education, many teens also engage in a variety of behaviors that place them at risk to either be injured, killed, or involved with the juvenile justice system. These are sometimes called *risk factors,* and include drug and alcohol use, underage drinking and smoking, drug dealing, the use of violence to solve problems with others, running away, truancy, dropping out of school, bringing weapons to school, vandalism, and theft. While some of these activities are considered typical teenage behaviors and are understood as part of a teen's search for identity and independence, they do place a youth at greater risk for getting into trouble.[17]

A related concept to understanding risky behaviors is what some psychologists call *the illusion of invulnerability.* This is the tendency of teenagers to believe that they are immune to the negative consequences of high-risk activities. This is not to say that youths do not recognize the risks associated with extreme behaviors, many do, but they often mistakenly believe that the potential or real consequences of those activities will not happen to them—that bad things happen to other people. The illusion of invulnerability suggests a belief by a particular teen that they possess some quality, trait, or characteristic that prevents them from being harmed, caught, or experiencing any negative consequence.[18]

Having identified many issues and problems confronting teenagers in the United States, most youths avoid getting into trouble, and if they do, their inappropriate behavior is sufficiently addressed and does not require further intervention on the part of the juvenile justice system. In fact, some youths who experience obstacles and pressures that place them at risk of engaging in delinquency somehow manage to overcome them and become productive and healthy adults. Much of the work on resiliency focuses on what are called *protective factors*, influences that shield or minimize the risk factors to which youths are exposed.[19]

The research on resiliency indicates that these characteristics can be identified and nurtured through the use of what researchers refer to as *developmental assets*. Experts believe that there are 40 developmental assets that allow youths to be resilient in the face of adversity.[20] Most youths possess about 12, but the more assets a youth possesses, the greater the likelihood he or she will be resilient. These assets consist of positive experiences, relationships, opportunities, and personal qualities that young people need to possess in order to grow up healthy, caring, and responsible.[21]

For example, research suggests that youths involved in constructive outlets during their free time are less likely to get involved in delinquency.[22] Additionally, spending time at home with family has a host of benefits, such as improving communication and developing positive relationships with parents. Thus, attachments to family, good friends, a safe school, and a concerned and committed larger community means youths can withstand peer pressure and avoid risky behaviors.[23]

Definitions of Juvenile Delinquency

As was mentioned, delinquency is a complex problem that requires a thorough understanding of the physical, social, economic, legal, and political context in which it occurs. Delinquency also encompasses a wide range of activities, resulting in considerable difficulty in adequately defining it. This is significant because how one defines delinquency has a lot to do with how it is measured, understood, and addressed. Sometimes the legal definition is used since it standardizes the behavior to some degree. However, the legal definition of delinquency is often different from what the general public or what parents might classify as a delinquent act.

Most states have some type of legal definition of delinquency that consists of behavior that violates the criminal code and is committed by a youth who has not reached majority age, usually 18.

Because each state decides on its own definition of delinquency, there is often wide variation in terms of how young or how old youths can be and still remain under the jurisdiction of the juvenile court. Table 1-1 offers a description of the youngest age at which an offender can be prosecuted (see Table 1-1).

Table 1-1
Lowest Age for Juvenile Court Jurisdiction
in Delinquency Matters by State*

Age 6	Age 7	Age 8	Age 10
North Carolina	Maryland	Arizona	Arkansas
	Massachusetts		Colorado
	New York		Kansas
			Louisiana
			Minnesota
			Mississippi
			Pennsylvania
			South
Dakota			
			Texas
			Vermont
			Wisconsin[24]

*Note: All other states have no specified lower age limit.

Historically, many states failed to make a distinction between criminal acts committed by youths and cases where youths were victims of abuse, neglect, or other mistreatment.[25] With the passage of federal legislation that separated minor offenders from serious ones, most notably the Juvenile Justice and Delinquency Prevention Act, many states began to distinguish between delinquents and status offenders, the latter of which are those who engaged in activity that could only be committed by youth, such as truancy, running away, or underage drinking.[26]

While legal definitions narrowly define certain acts as delinquent, suggesting that delinquency consists of only those instances in which youths have been arrested and adjudicated for a crime, others define delinquency much more broadly. Parents and siblings, for example, may use the term *delinquent* to define a wide array of behaviors, such as a youth who refuses to clean his room, complete his household chores, who hangs out with people his parents think are troublemakers, or who listens to rap music. How a youth dresses, talks, and with whom he or she associates do not necessarily mean he or she has broken any laws. While parents may complain to social workers, counselors, or even probation officers, these types of behaviors are not likely to be considered by the juvenile justice system. The wide range of activities also suggests that there is a great deal of interpretation and subjectivity associated with delinquency. How behavior and offenders are perceived, positively or negatively, is an important consideration in the study of delinquency.

As was mentioned, during the 1980s and 1990s, there was a perception by many politicians and policymakers that not only was serious juvenile crime increasing, but also the juvenile justice system was too lenient with offenders. In response, many states attempted to limit the authority of the juvenile court over some types of delinquents. Some changes included mandatory waivers and/or mandatory sentences for certain offenses; a reduction in protections normally afforded to juveniles, such as confidentiality laws, fingerprinting and photographing suspects during booking procedures; using a juvenile's prior record at the sentencing stage of the process; and allowing juvenile hearings to be open to the public.

Over the past 30 years, media images of juveniles as violence-prone and chronic offenders along with claims by policymakers and politicians that delinquency is out of control, has created an image of the modern-day delinquent. However, the evidence clearly shows that the vast majority of juvenile offenders are not violent, nor chronic in their misbehavior, and the juvenile justice system appears to be able to adequately deal with the challenges that juvenile offenders present to their respective communities.[27]

As we will discuss in subsequent chapters, there is also ample research to suggest that incarceration does not rehabilitate juvenile offenders.[28] In fact, it can result in contributing to the delinquency problem, as youths are more likely to commit additional crimes after being incarcerated.[29]

Delinquency and Public Policy

Much of what we do about a problem like delinquency will be shaped by how it is perceived as well as how it is defined. As we have seen, part of the shaping of public policy regarding delinquency has been that policymakers and politicians have their own ideas about the extent and seriousness of the problem despite the fact that the general public does not feel the same way about juvenile offenders. Similarly, policy will also be shaped on how the problem is defined. If we continue to dedicate resources to avenues that target violent offenders, one can only conclude that this is how delinquency is understood. However, as we will see in the chapters ahead, many of the programs designed to treat and rehabilitate juvenile offenders do just that, but they are often underfunded or overlooked because violent offenders get more media attention.

That being said, there are a number of special populations that compose the delinquency population that are often overlooked. Even in these instances, however, there is ample evidence that effective treatment can be beneficial and even result in a reduction in repeated behavior. While most of the literature points out that the vast majority of delinquents do not become chronic offenders, nor do they progress to criminal careers as adults, some youths do choose that path. Part of the purpose of this book is to show that even the most extreme forms of delinquency, including sex offenders, fire starters, and some forms of violent offenders, can be treated. The result is that these offenders can go on to become productive citizens.

In the next chapter we discuss perhaps one of the most misunderstood segments of the delinquency population: juvenile sex offenders. Given that their adult counterparts receive an inordinate amount of attention when they victimize children, it seems pertinent to note that juveniles who engage in a wide range of sex offenses are very different from adults, both in terms of their motivations, characteristics, and amenability to treatment.

In Chapter 3 we focus on another type of sex offender: juvenile prostitutes. As we discuss, much of this activity characterizes offenders more as victims rather than perpetrators of crime. The vast majority of juvenile prostitutes become involved in the trade due to neglect or abuse at home. Once on the street, however, there are few opportunities for them to earn a living and prostitution often becomes a means of survival.

In the second section of the book we discuss issues relating to mental illness and delinquency. The issue of mental illness impacts delinquency in a number of ways, primarily in terms of understanding these types of offenders from a medical model. In Chapter 4 we explore an understudied area of delinquency: juvenile fire-starting, which although illegal, is a manifestation of other problems. This chapter is dedicated to not only understanding the nature of fire setting behavior, but also the most effective treatment methods available.

Chapter 5 examines juvenile domestic violence. While this might normally be categorized as a form of violent crimes/offenders, given that much of the literature focuses on the background factors and other psychological issues stemming from parental abuse, sibling violence, and dating violence, we have included it under the section on mental illness.

Section three of this book focuses on chronic offenders. It is this category that likely receives the most attention in the media, particularly as it relates to violent offenders. Chapter 6 discusses the nature of violent chronic offending, including gang violence and what is known as *the career criminal*. As was mentioned, while the vast majority of youths do not become involved in criminal activities and while most delinquents do not go on to become adult offenders (or even repeat offenders as youths), this segment of the juvenile offender population is the exception to that rule. Included in the discussion on violent offenders is an examination of the reasons for the violence and the corresponding value system that perpetuates it.

Finally, in Chapter 7 we look at the other side of chronic offending—those who are non-violent but persistent offenders. These youths tend to be involved in more property-related activities and while the harm and damage they cause can be considerable, much of the debate centers around whether or not these activities are simply normal teenage behavior taken to an unhealthy degree. Included in this chapter is a discussion of computer hacking, vandalism/graffiti, underage drinking, and underage smoking. While the latter two are considered status offenses and not as serious as the other two, the costs to society and to the individuals involved are considerable and warrant discussion.

As a whole, this book is designed to explain and help the reader understand the different dimensions of delinquency not typically discussed in a traditional delinquency textbook or in a course on juvenile delinquency. It is our hope that by shedding light on these populations and the reasons behind their activities, a greater understanding of delinquency in general can be obtained. In many ways, these offenders are similar to most youths—the differences that exist are often understandable, explainable, and even treatable. However, in order for this to occur, the public's perception of these offenders and delinquents in general, must be understood in its proper context. Hopefully, we have accomplished that goal here.

Summary

It seems clear that the size of the adolescent population, those under the age of 18, is growing and will continue to do so well into the next several decades. The presence of such a sizeable group presents a number of challenges for parents, politicians, policymakers, and officials in the juvenile justice system. Part of the challenge is that the perception of youths is colored by a belief that most of them are willing and able to engage in delinquency and violence.

While the public has become fearful of youthful offenders, they still believe in the idea of rehabilitation over punishment. Many polls demonstrate that the public does not believe that treating youths like adults will solve the problems relating to delinquency. On the other hand, policymakers and politicians think punishment is needed and have changed many laws regarding delinquency. Such changes include mandatory waivers to adult court, greater discretion by prosecutors in deciding whether to handle a juvenile case informally or whether to waive it to adult court, and greater use of detention for delinquents, even those who are not violent offenders.

Much of the discussion of the different types of offenders outlined in the chapters of this book serve to demystify the nature of the activities and the motivations for participating in this form of criminal behavior. While some individuals knowingly and intentionally engage in illegal behaviors because of the benefits or because they think they can get away with it, in most cases there is usually a particular reason behind the activity; sometimes it is the result of a psychological disorder or the result of childhood trauma.

Notes

1. Krisberg, B. and S. Marchionna. 2007. *Attitudes of U.S. Voters toward Youth Crime and the Justice System.* Washington, DC: National Council on Crime and Delinquency. Available at http:// www.nccd-crc.org/nccd/ pubs/zogby_feb07.pdf.

2. Ibid.

3. Ibid.

4. National Juvenile Justice Network. 2009. *Polling on Public Attitudes About Treatment of Young Offenders.* Washington, DC. Available at http://www.njjn.org/media/resources/public/resource _633. pdf See also *Rehabilitation Versus Incarceration of Juvenile Offenders: Public Preferences in Four Models for Change States,* http://modelsforchange.net/pdfs/WillingnesstoPayFINAL.pdf.

See also Nagin, D. S. and Piquero, A. R. 2006. "Public Preferences for Rehabilitation Versus Incarceration of Juvenile Offenders: Evidence from a Contingent Valuation Survey." *Criminology & Public Policy,* 5(4), November. See also, National Council on Crime and Delinquency, 2007. See also Mears, D. P.; Carter, J. Gertz, M. and Mancini, C. 2007. "Public Opinion and the Foundation of the Juvenile Court." *Criminology,* 45(1): 57–79.

5. See for instance *Report of the Virginia Commission on Youth on the Study of Juvenile Justice System Reform,* House Document No. 37(1996); Soler, M. 1999. *Public Opinion on Youth, Crime and*

Race: A Guide for Advocates. Washington, DC: Building Blocks for Youth, http://www.buildingblocksforyouth.org/ advocacyguide.pdf.

6. National Juvenile Justice Network, 2009.

7. Juvenile Violent Offenders—The Concept Of The Juvenile Super Predator http://law.jrank.org/pages/1546/Juvenile-Violent-Offenders-concept-juvenile-super-predator.html#ixzz0auiTs8YR.

8. Ibid.

9. Marrus, E. 2007. *Children and Juvenile Justice.* Durham, NC: Carolina Academic Press.

10. Ibid.

11. Ibid.

12. Yanich, D. 2005. "Kids, Crime, and Local Television News." *Crime and Delinquency* 51(1): 103–132.; see also Goidel, R. K., Freeman, C. M., and Procopio, S. T. 2006. "The Impact of Television Viewing on Perceptions of Juvenile Crime." *Journal of Broadcast and Electronic Media,* March, 1–19. Gilliam, F., and Iyengar, S. 2001. "Prime suspects: The influence of Local Television News on the Viewing Public." *American Journal of Political Science,* 44: 560–573.; Gilliam, F., and Iyengar, S. 2000. "Super-predators or Victims of Societal Neglect? Framing Effects in Juvenile Crime Coverage." In K. Callaghan and F. Schnell (eds.), *The Framing of American Politics,* 148–166). Pittsburgh: University of Pittsburgh Press.

13. Ibid. See also Cottle, J. and Perrault, R. 2009. "The Juvenile Delinquent Stereotype." Paper presented at the American Psychology-Law Society, San Antonio, TX.

14. Gilliam, F., and Bales, S. 2003. "Strategic Frame Analysis: Reframing America's Youth." *Social Policy Report,* 15: 3–21.

15. Busselle, R. W. 2001. "Television Exposure, Perceived Realism, and Exemplar Accessibility in Social Judgment Process." *Media Psychology,* 3: 43–68. Busselle, R. W., and Shrum, L. J. 2003. "Media Exposure and Exemplar Accessibility." *Media Psychology,* 5: 255–282. Zillmann & Brosius, 2000.

16. Tamborini, R., Zillmann, D., and Bryant, J. 1984. "Fear and Victimization: Exposure to Television and Perceptions of Crime and Fear." In R. N. Bostrom (ed.), *Communication Yearbook,* 492–513. Beverly Hills, CA: Sage.; Taylor, D. G., Scheppele, K. L., and Stinchcombe, A. L. 1979. "Salience of Crime and Sup-

port for Harsher Criminal Sanctions." *Social Problems*, 26: 413–424.; Weaver, J., & Wakshlag, J. 1986. "Perceived Vulnerability to Crime, Criminal Victimization Experience and Television Viewing." *Journal of Broadcasting and Electronic Media*, 30: 141–155. Wilson, B. J., Colvin, C. M., and Smith, S. 2002. "Engaging in Violence on American Television: A Comparison of Child, Teen and Adult Perpetrators." *Journal of Communication*, 52: 36–60.

17. Shader, M. 2007. *Risk Factors for Delinquency: An Overview.* Washington DC: U.S. Department of Justice, Office of Justice Programs, Office of Juvenile Justice and Delinquency Prevention. Available at http://www.ncjrs.gov/pdffiles1/ojjdp/frd030 127.pdf.

18. Sagarin, B. J., Cialdini, R. B., Rice, W. E., Serna, S. B. 2002. "Dispelling the Illusion of Invulnerability: the Motivations and Mechanisms of Resistance to Persuasion." *Journal of Personality and Social Psychology*, 83(3): 526–541.

19. Goldstein, S., & Brooks, R. (eds.). 2005. *Handbook of Resilience in Children.* New York: Kluver Academic Press.

20. Ibid.

21. See for instance Luthar, S. S. 2006. *Resilience in Development: A Synthesis of Research Across Five Decades.* New York: John Wiley and Sons. See also Elias, M. (2008, March). Laws of Life: A Literacy-Based Intervention for Social-Emotional and Character Development and Resilience. *Perspectives in Education, 26,* 75–79. Heller, S. S., Larrieu, J. A., D'Imperio, R,. and Boris, N. W. 1999. "Research on Resiliency to Child Maltreatment: Empirical Considerations. *Child Abuse and Neglect* 23(4): 321–338.See discussion of developmental assets and how to nurture their development at http://www.search-institute.org/.

22. Ibid.

23. Search Institute brochure. http://www.search-institute. org/ accessed July 15, 2008.

24. King, M. and Szymanski, L. 2006. "National Overview," *State Juvenile Justice Profiles.* Pittsburg, PA: National Center on Juvenile Justice. Available at http://www.ncjj.org/state/profiles/.

25. Juvenile Justice and Delinquency Prevention Act of 1974 P.L. 93–415, 88 Stat. 1109.

26. See McNamara, R. H. 2008. *The Lost Population: Status Offenders in America.* Durham, NC: Carolina Academic Press.

27. Marrus, 2007.

28. See Mendel, R. A. 2002. *Less Hype, More Help: Reducing Juvenile Crime: What Works and What Doesn't.* Washington, DC: America Youth Forum; also Krisberg, B. 2005. *Juvenile Justice: Redeeming our Children.* Los Angeles: Sage; Mackenzie, D. L. 2006. *What Works in Corrections.* Boston, MA: Cambridge University Press, 271–303.

29. Ibid.

Chapter 2

Juvenile Sex Offenders

Case Studies in Delinquency

Austin is a thirteen-year-old boy who was arrested and charged with possession of child pornography. Austin's girlfriend, who was just about to turn twelve and wanted to celebrate her birthday, took a nude photo of herself and sent it to Austin's phone as a text message. At the time, Austin was watching his school's basketball team playing a game in the school gymnasium. Standing next to him was a teacher, who happened to be at the game. When he opened the message on his phone, the teacher saw the nude photo, confiscated the phone and had Austin arrested. Because his girlfriend is a minor, Austin was charged under the child pornography statutes and adjudicated a delinquent. As a result of a plea agreement, he was sentenced to two years' probation and had his name listed on the registry for sexual offenders. He also agreed to participate in an outpatient treatment program for juvenile sex offenders. In his home state, South Carolina, he will remain on the sexual offender registry for life.

Questions to Consider:

1. Should the teacher have handled the situation differently? What other options were available?
2. Are the girlfriend's parents responsible for her behavior?
3. Did Austin do anything wrong and should he be charged with a crime?

It is perhaps one of the greatest fears of parents: the sexual victimization of their child. Few events evoke a more emotional reaction by parents and the public alike. Images of pedophiles roaming the streets in search of a victim create a climate of fear, hostility, and in extreme cases, vigilante responses. While the subject of adult sexual offenders has received a great deal of media attention, particularly in light of the numerous cases of Catholic priests victimizing young boys in the United States, there is another dimension to sexual offending that must be considered: juvenile sex offenders (JSOs). Part of the challenge in addressing the issues and problems stemming from juvenile sex offenders is distinguishing them from their adult counterparts. There are important differences between adult and juvenile sex offenders that should be noted—in many ways these are two separate and distinct populations. In addition, there are a number of myths associated with JSOs, in part because of the perception of the connection to adult offending.

Still another challenge in the study of JSOs is the emphasis on punishment instead of treatment for offenders. As was mentioned in the opening chapter, Americans have embarked upon a "get tough" strategy for delinquents despite the fact that this approach is contradictory to the philosophy of the juvenile court and is largely ineffective in changing behavior. Given the emotions swirling around this type of activity, it makes sense that the public would focus less on helping offenders and more on punishing them. However, the costs of treatment are much lower than incarceration. According to the U.S. Department of Justice's Center for Sex Offender Management, one year of intensive supervision and treatment can range between $5,000 and $15,000 depending on the type of treatment used. However, the costs of incarceration for a juvenile offender are over $20,000 per year.[1] Thus, placing youths in a detention facility without any form of treatment likely means offenders will serve their sentences and be released into the community—where their sexually abusive behavior will likely reoccur. There is also evidence that effective sex offender treatment interventions can reduce future sexual misconduct to some degree.

Defining a Juvenile Sex Offender

While it might seem easy to classify JSOs—individuals who commit sex offenses—the problem of classification emerges when one considers the wide range of behaviors such a definition includes. While many people might think of a sex offense as an aggressive sexual assault or rape, sexual crimes also include statutory rape, voyeurism, exhibitionism, obscene phone calls, and a wide range of other sexual activities. The matter is complicated further by the age of the offender.

On one hand, classifying sex offenders might seem to be a simple matter, particularly if an adult commits a sex crime against a minor. But what if the victim was willing to participate in the sexual activity but was too young to grant consent? What if the offender was an adult and the age difference between the victim and the offender was small? Such is often the case in statutory rape cases. Thus, while it may seem easy to classify sex offenders as either adults or juveniles, there is a great deal more complexity to the problem than what might appear at first glance.

At one end of the spectrum are children—legally, a person is considered a child when, by virtue of his or her immaturity, he or she cannot be held responsible for their behavior. In most states, a person younger than 12 years of age is considered to be a child. In general, the law recognizes that a child is unable to possess the capacity to understand the potential outcome of a particular behavior. This means they cannot form criminal intent, an essential component of a crime.[2]

Legally, a juvenile is an individual who is under a certain legal age at which he or she would be charged as an adult for a criminal act.[3] In the majority of states in the United States and in most other Western jurisdictions, a person is considered to be an adult when he or she reaches the age of 18. Other states classify a person an adult when they are 16 or 17 years old in some circumstances.[4]

A juvenile sex offender then is a person who has been convicted of a sexual offense and who is considered to be old enough to be held criminally liable for the crime, but not so old as to be treated like an adult. Another term often used interchangeably with juvenile sex offenders is *adolescent sex offender*. Adolescence is defined as the period of physical and psychological development from the onset of puberty to maturity. Typically, puberty is reached between the ages of 13 and 16 for boys and 11 and 14 years of age for girls.[5] Strictly speaking then, a youth who has committed a sexual crime but has not yet reached puberty would be a juvenile offender, and one who commits the act after the onset of puberty would be an adolescent sex offender.

However, in the social science literature, the term *juvenile sex offender* has become the label of choice to describe the behaviors and age groups discussed thus far. These distinctions highlight the ways in which some organizations define sexual offenders. For instance, according to the National Adolescent Perpetrator Network, an adolescent sex offender is a "youth ranging from puberty to the age of legal majority who commits any sexual interaction with a person of any age against the victim's will, without consent, or in an aggressive, exploitative, or threatening manner."[6] For our purposes, we will incorporate both juveniles and adolescents into our definition and say that a JSO is either a juvenile or an adolescent who commits any sexual interaction with a person of any age against the victim's will, and who, in the commission of such crimes, acts in an aggressive, exploitative, or threatening manner towards their victims.

Juvenile Sex Offending versus Problem Behaviors

What about young children who engage in inappropriate sexual behaviors? While legally the state might not prosecute them, they still constitute a set of challenges and problems for parents and communities. Thus, in addition to a discussion about JSOs, we should also point out how younger children who engage in sexualized behaviors are categorized. Specifically, a child under 12 years old who engages in sexual behavior, either with him or herself or involving others is referred to as having sexual behavior problems (SBPs). According to the National Center on Sexual Behavior of Youth, SBPs are attributed to those children under the age of 12 who "demonstrate developmentally inappropriate or aggressive sexual behavior."[7] This could include self-sexual behavior such as masturbation or aggressive sexual behavior towards others. Because this is a relatively new area of research, there are a host of misconceptions about SBPs. While some people might consider all sexual behavior between children a normal part of their development, the research suggests that if such behavior occurs frequently, involves coercion, causes emotional distress or occurs between children of significantly different ages, clinicians consider this to be problematic.[8]

Research has also shown that, contrary to popular belief, children with SBPs are often females, who have not been sexually abused. Factors such as exposure to family violence, family sexuality patterns that foster intimate touching, and access to sexually charged material, among other variables, play a significant role in explaining SBPs. Fortunately, like JSOs, the data shows that children with SBPs can be effectively treated without institutional care and that most children with SBPs do not grow up to be adult sexual offenders.[9]

Myths about Sex Offenders

As was mentioned, there are several myths surrounding juvenile sex offending. For example, one myth suggests that strangers commit sexual assaults. This is a common misperception by the public of all crimes—in reality people known by or acquainted with the victim commit most crimes. In fact, approximately 60% of boys and 80% of girls who are sexually abused are victimized by relatives, friends, babysitters, or people who supervise them. The evidence shows that these individuals, perhaps the closest to the child, are more likely than strangers to victimize them sexually.[10]

Another myth perpetuated in the media is that sexual exploitation is on the increase. Despite the extensive media coverage of events such as those involving the Catholic Church, according to the Uniform Crime Reports, the rate of reported rape (one of the lowest for all crimes) among women has remained virtually the same between 2000 and 2007 (90,178 offenses in 2000 compared to 90,427 in 2007) and decreased in 2009 (88,097 offenses).[11] Additionally, the arrest rate for all sexual offenses, including forcible rape and not including prostitution, decreased 18% between 2000 and 2007 (27,469 arrests in 2000 compared to 23,307 in 2007), according to the Uniform Crime Reports.[12] This trend continued in 2009 where only 21,407 arrests were made.[13]

Still another myth about sexual offending is the belief that children who are sexually assaulted will commit that same crime against others when they are adults. While the risks of sexually aggressive behavior are higher if the person has been sexually abused, most children who were abused do not inflict that same trauma on others. Some studies show that JSOs have higher rates of sexual abuse in their histories than the general population. However, rates of physical and sexual abuse vary widely for JSOs: 20–50% have experienced physical abuse and 40–80% have experienced sexual abuse. Still, while many JSOs have histories of being abused, the majority do not go on to commit sex crimes as adults.[14]

Finally, there is a popular misconception that sex offenders cannot be effectively treated. Just as there is no single type of sex offender, there is no single type of treatment method. Perhaps most important, not everyone responds to treatment in the same ways. There is some evidence that suggests treatment programs that are comprehensive in scope, empirically based, and target a particular type of offense, can be effective. Generally, the research indicates that effective programs can achieve a reduction in recidivism for some types of JSOs. The research also shows that those who fail to complete treatment programs are at much greater risk for committing a higher rate of all types of offenses.[15]

Differences between Adult and Juvenile Sex Offenders

Because of a number of celebrated cases where adults have exploited children, such as the charges against former pop singer Michael Jackson,[16] as well as the exploitation of young boys by members of the Catholic church,[17] it is easy to conclude that all sex offenders are alike. However, sex offenders come from a wide range of backgrounds and engage in a considerable array of activities. This makes the study of sex offenders a difficult task. Added to this complexity are the differences between adult sex offenders and their juvenile counterparts. The latter are not simply smaller and younger versions of adult offenders: there are significant differences between adult sex offenders and JSOs. For example, compared to adults who sexually offend, juveniles have fewer victims and are generally less aggressive in their sexual offenses. Additionally, most JSOs are not sexual predators, do not meet the definition of a pedophile (defined as a person who fantasizes about or engages in sexual activity with prepubescent children),[18] and do not have the same long-term behavioral tendencies as adults.[19]

The research also suggests that, compared to adult sex offenders, juveniles are generally less likely to commit additional sex crimes if they have received treatment. The overall sex offense recidivism rate for juveniles is between 5% and 15%, depending on the behavior, which is quite low. Juveniles who successfully complete sexual offender treatment have also been found to have a lower recidivism rate than their untreated counterparts.[20]

Statistics on Juvenile Sex Offenders

As was mentioned, one of the challenges to studying juvenile sex offending is that offenders come from a wide range of backgrounds and engage in a host of different sexual crimes. This makes drawing any broad conclusions about sex offenders a significant challenge. In 2007, The National Center on Sexual Behavior of Youth found that adolescent sex offenders accounted for approximately one-third of all reported sex offenses against children.[21]

According to the Bureau of Justice Statistics, in 2006:

- 23% of all sexual assault offenders were under age 18 at the time of the offense.
- About 4% were under the age of 12.
- The age at which most offenses are committed is 14 years old.
- Nearly 80% have a diagnosable psychiatric disorder.
- Up to half have histories of physical abuse.
- Up to 80% have histories of sexual abuse.[22]

Estimates of sexual abuse among JSOs indicate they are three to four times more likely to have been sexually abused than male adolescents in the general population.[23]

Additionally, the research suggests a trend between academic achievement and sex offending: between 30–60% of juvenile sex offenders demonstrate some type of learning disability and low academic achievement.[24] It should also be noted that sex crimes are not the only type of delinquent activity juvenile sex offenders engage in, but if a youth engages in sexual offending, he or she is also more likely to become involved in other forms of delinquency.[25]

It is important to note that research suggests many sex offenses committed by children are not violent crimes—in fact, most child sex offenders do not engage in aggressive or violent behavior. In one study of child sexual offenders, 59% were categorized as touching or fondling and 14% were classified for what is described as *non-contact offenses*, such as indecent exposure. The remaining 27% of cases consisted of rape. Additionally, in rape cases where the offender is under 18 years of age, the victim is likely to have been the same age as the perpetrator or older.[26]

Furthermore, as was mentioned, while the empirical evidence on chronic sex offending by youths either during adolescence or after they become adults is limited, the weight of the evidence suggests that most juvenile sex offenders do not progress into chronic offending as adults.[27] For instance, one study of recidivism of 300 male sex offenders in the United States who committed sex offenses when they were children found that only 4% had committed another sex offense three to six years after they were released from custody.[28]

Similarly, a study of 204 male child sex offenders and 41 female child sex offenders in Philadelphia found that only 10% of the boys committed another sex offense within eight years of their 18th birthday and none of the female offenders committed another sex offense in the same period.[29] The study also showed that having committed a sex offense as a juvenile was not a particularly strong predictor of committing a sex offense as an adult.[30]

As was mentioned, very few adult sex offenders have convictions for similar types of offenses as children. This runs counter to the notion that all adult sex offenders begin their crimes early and never stop. In one study, only 8% of adult sex offenders had been juvenile sex offenders,[31] while another study found it was half that number, 4%.[32] This finding is important because it raises questions about the value and need to require juveniles to register as sex offenders, a topic to which we will turn later in this chapter.

A Typology of Juvenile Sex Offenders

Because of the recent interest in JSOs, and because it encompasses a wide range of activities, researchers have made attempts to classify the various activities and offenders in this population. For instance, some experts have created typologies based on the characteristics of the offense. One researcher found that child molesters have different rates of arousal than rapists, who are more likely to be aggressive in their behavioral patterns.

By grouping offenders into three categories: aggressive offenses (such as sexual assault and rape), hands-off offenses (such as voyeurism, exhibitionism and obscene phone calls), and pedophiliac offenses (offenses against young children), researchers found that the aggressive offenses' group had higher rates of delinquency and violence as well as lower IQ levels. The hands-off group was described as impulsive but not violent. Offenders in this category were not as experienced sexually. The pedophiliac offenders also had high rates of delinquency, but had poor relationships with parents and unstable home lives.[33]

Another way to organize sex offenders is by the cognitive capabilities of the offender. These typologies demonstrate differences in how offenders process information and how they have developed individually rather than simply how they act. One of the most comprehensive typologies of JSOs is known as the PHASE typology. It defines six categories of offenders:

Naïve Experimenter/Abuser. This category consists of younger offenders (age 11–13) whose offenses do not involve the use of force or threats and typically involve victimizing a young child (age 2–6). This type of offender is experimenting and exploring his sexual feelings.

The Under-Socialized Child Exploiter. This type of offender is more likely to be a chronic offender who victimizes young children, but the motivations are not a result of experimentation. Rather, they occur because the offender feels isolated, alone, and has a need for self-identity. Typically offenders in this category use manipulation or trickery to exploit their victims.

The Pseudo-Socialized Child Exploiter. This is generally an older adolescent who appears to be psychologically well-balanced and "normal." However, this type of offender does not show any guilt or remorse over their actions, and his or her own sexual needs are more important than anything that might happen to their victims.

Sexually Aggressive. These offenders typically come from abusive families and tend to use force or threats. The motive for this type of offender is to control the victim or to exert power over them. Interestingly, these types of offenders can be charming and have good social skills. This is the type of offender that the public is most concerned about because of the willingness to use force on victims.

Sexual Compulsive. These types of offenders usually engage in more passive behaviors such as voyeurism, obscene phone calls, or exhibitionism. Offenders in this category typically come from rigid and inflexible families and tend to be compulsive in their behaviors. The motivation behind their sexual offending is to relieve the anxiety in other parts of their lives or to experience the thrill and excitement of risky activity.

Group Influence Offender. This group consists of those who are motivated by peer pressure or who attempt to gain status with their peers. They are largely dependent upon friends and colleagues for their sense of identity and usually co-offend with another peer present.[34]

It is clear from this typology that the motivations for committing the various sexual offenses are different, calling attention to the need for different types of treatment plans and environments based on the severity and particular offenses.

Case Study
What Do We Make of Austin's Situation?

Given what you have read thus far, what can we say about Austin's situation? He was charged with possession of child pornography, since his girlfriend was eleven years old at the time of the event. This crime is normally considered a felony and carries with it a lengthy mandatory sentence. However, despite the fact that he did not know his girlfriend was going to send the photo, Austin was still adjudicated a delinquent and required to participate in therapy for sex offenders. When he began attending the program, Austin suddenly refused to participate, arguing he was not like other patients and he had been wrongly convicted in the first place. His probation officer told him that his full sentence would be carried out if he did not comply with the criteria set out in his probation agreement.

As a result of his conviction, Austin was expelled from school and the community reaction to the situation was angry and swift—families did not want him around their children and his church pastor told him he could no longer attend services with that congregation. Is Austin a sex offender? Will treatment serve any useful purpose? Will he likely become an adult offender, as his teachers and classmates have predicted?

Juvenile Female Sex Offenders

While the study of male sex offenders has received considerable attention, a number of celebrated cases of schoolteachers who engaged in inappropriate sexual behavior with male students have brought increased attention to female sex offenders.[35] However, the research on this topic is scant.

The motives for female sex offenders may be very different than those for male sex offenders, and researchers are still developing their understanding of this population. According to a recent report on female sex offenders by the Center for Sex Offender Management, part of the problem relates to the reliability of information on this population—there is no single database from which to draw information.[36] Consequently, researchers draw from a variety of sources, such as the Uniform Crime Reports, the NCVS, and self-report data, all of which are limited in their scope and comprehensiveness.

According to the 2009 Uniform Crime Reports (UCR), of adults and juveniles who came to the attention of the police for sex crimes, females accounted for less than 10% of these cases. Specifically, arrests of women represent only about 1% of all adult arrests for forcible rape and 9% of all adult arrests for other sex offenses.[37] As it relates to juveniles, the data from juvenile court suggests that females are responsible for about 3% of forcible rape cases, about 5% of other violent sex offenses, and 19% of non-violent sex offenses.[38]

More alarming is the trend in arrest data. While arrests of adult women for sex offenses decreased in recent years, the number of adolescent girls coming to the attention of the juvenile courts for sex offenses has increased significantly. Between 1997 and 2002, the most recent period for which data is available, juvenile cases involving female-perpetrated forcible rapes rose by 6%. Other violent sex offenses increased by 62% and non-violent sex offenses rose by 42%.[39] If the information on juvenile trends is reliable, female involvement in juvenile sex-related crimes has increased substantially.

While data from the UCR consistently shows that females are involved in a small number of sex offenses, an examination of victimization surveys, such as the National Crime Victimization Survey (NCVS), shows the incidence of female-perpetrated sex crimes is often higher and much more variable. For example, victimization data reveal that up to 63% of female victims and as many as 27% of male victims report having been sexually victimized by a female. In addition, although the NCVS indicates that females represent up to 6% of rapes or sexual assaults by an individual acting alone, it also implicates female offenders in up to 40% of sex crimes involving multiple offenders.[40]

As was mentioned, the data on female sex offenders in general is limited, but information on female juvenile sex offenders is even more obscure. What can be derived from several studies of this population is that female juvenile sex offenders have been the victims of sexual abuse themselves; have dysfunctional families; suffer from a number of psychological disorders, including post-traumatic stress disorder (PTSD); tend to target young children, usually within the family; and tend to act alone.[41]

In terms of creating a typology of female juvenile sex offenders, similar to the one offered for males, one might consider the following as a guide to understanding the different degrees of female sex offending:

Experimenters. This type of female sex offender often engages in a small number of incidents within the context of babysitting. This type of offender is relatively inexperienced and naïve, and their motivation for engaging in the activity is due to curiosity more than any other reason. This type of offender does not have a long history of abuse, family discord, or other psychological problems.

Mirrors. This type of female offender consists of young women who are sexually active, and while they may suffer from some type of emotional or psychological problem, it is not severe or debilitating. In fact, many of these girls have adequate social skills and appear to be emotionally balanced. This type of offender commits sexual acts against young children that mirror their own victimization as children.

Chronic Abusers. These types of female sex offenders engage in extensive sex offending and have high levels of emotional and psychosexual trauma, usually the result of being victimized at an early age. This group is likely to be in need of significant treatment and counseling. They are also most likely to be incarcerated. This group has a long history of family abuse and a host of other problems.[42]

Differences between Male and Female Sex Offenders

The research on the characteristics of female juvenile sex offenders suggests that they are very similar in some ways to their male counterparts. Both groups demonstrate a history of family difficulties, poor coping skills, low self-esteem, substance abuse, and difficulty in sustaining intimate relationships with others.[43] There are, however, some noted differences between male and female juvenile sex offenders. For instance, the history of sexual abuse among female juvenile offenders is greater and longer in duration compared to males. Females are also more likely to commit a sexual offense while providing care of some type to their victim, such as a child. This relates to another difference between male and female juvenile offenders: women are more likely than males to victimize young children. With older victims, rape is less likely to occur with females compared to men, but when it does occur, the act is usually a same sex crime, with women victimizing other women.[44]

Thus, the study and treatment of sex offenders in the United States has focused primarily on male offenders, and while historically female sex offenders have been overlooked by officials in the criminal and juvenile justice system, recent research on this population is beginning to shed light on the extent, type, and treatment of female juvenile sex offenders.[45]

Explaining Juvenile Sex Offending

There is a great deal of debate concerning why sexual offenders, particularly juveniles, engage in these types of activities. Some experts even wonder if sexual offending is reflective of some other problem. On one hand, the numerous theories explaining why people become adult sex offenders are extended to JSOs. They include genetic explanations, where some experts point to the fact that sex offenders have higher testosterone levels, which ultimately results in criminal offenses.[46] Other experts point to environmental factors, where children who witness or experience sexual abuse are more likely to abuse others. Officials at the Safer Society Foundation, a non-profit organization that attempts to protect children from predators, argue that a number of children who engage in sexual offending have learned how to commit sex acts as well as how to justify them. Because this behavior is learned, it is possible to teach and counsel offenders on another course of action through behavior modification therapy. Another learning theory explanation is that sex offending, especially as it relates to pedophiles, occurs because offenders never learned appropriate responses or skills needed to carry on constructive relationships with others.

On the other hand, many experts argue that the deep-seated psychological problems seen in adult sexual offenders are not applicable to juveniles. Some experts point to studies that identify "non-sexual problems" as the most important factor behind serious sex crimes by child offenders.[47] According to the Association for the Treatment of Sexual Abusers:

> Poor social competency skills and deficits in self-esteem can best explain sexual deviance in children, rather than paraphilic *[an abnormal or an unnatural attraction—emphasis mine]* interests and psychopathic characteristics that are more common in adult offenders. There is little evidence that ... these youths engage in acts of sexual penetration for the same reasons as their adult counterparts.[48]

Thus, in many respects, we should take care in adequately distinguishing between adult sex offenders and JSOs: clearly the motives for offending are different; the patterns of victimization, and the explanations for their behavior are different from adult offenders. Perhaps most important is the notion that, unlike adult sex offenders, JSOs are amenable to treatment, meaning their behavior is correctable in many instances.[49]

Treatment of Juvenile Sex Offenders

In the past thirty years, much has been learned about the treatment of JSOs. In the early 1980s, when therapy on this population was in its early stages, one approach was to simply take the treatment model used on adult sex offenders and apply it to juveniles. Some treatment plans were based on the notion that sex, like drugs, was an addiction. In this model, offenders would need to be mindful of triggering events, such as viewing pornography, that could cause a relapse. One early treatment strategy was to have JSOs keep journals where they detailed their fantasies about sex. The therapist, after reading the journal, would outline a "relapse-prevention plan" to avoid a cycle of re-offending.[50]

This model, sometimes referred to as *the trickle down treatment approach,* was an ineffective way to help JSOs. Like many early treatment modalities, the trickle down approach failed to appreciate the developmental differences between JSOs and adult sex offenders as well as the differences in motive and scope of activities between the two groups. Thus, the approach of treating juvenile sex offenders as mini-adults resulted in less successful treatment programs for youth.[51]

More recently, while there are a host of treatment options for JSOs, generally speaking the treatment of JSOs can be understood in terms of accountability and awareness. That is, the process of any treatment strategy begins with breaking through the denial and helping the individual assume responsibility for his or her actions. A large part of that process involves making the offender aware that he or she made a choice to act inappropriately, no matter how many risk factors the individual faced. Whatever errors in thinking and processing that may have occurred, the individual must learn to recognize them as well as wanting to effect changes. Treatment experts argue that there is a delicate balance between accepting responsibility and recognizing the ability to change. This can be accomplished by separating the offense from the offender.[52]

The second part of the goal of treatment is to increase the youth's awareness of his or her tendencies and to find alternative ways to correct them. In other words, the youth needs to learn the triggering mechanisms that caused the behavior in the first place. He or she also needs to experience guilt and remorse about what was done to the victim and construct strategies that prevent the negative thoughts from becoming victimizing behavior. More concretely, treatment typically involves teaching youths how to slow down their reactions to stimuli, which gives them time to control their impulsiveness and anger, thereby defusing rage and destructive tendencies. This can occur through such techniques as self-talk, thought stopping, and distraction through other activities.[53]

Another suggestion is to have sexual offenders write an autobiography. This exercise encourages youths to process previous experiences, which they may not have considered in a long while. In the process, they may learn the roots of their fear, inadequacy, inferiority, low self-esteem, and immaturity.

Treatment can take many forms: lectures, discussions, exercises, role-playing, and the aforementioned journaling, to name a few examples. Role-playing in particular is seen by experts as particularly effective in helping to break down denial, in arousing social sensitivity, as well as developing an ability to empathize with others. The general consensus among mental health professionals is that group therapy is particularly effective for JSOs. The reason is that the group has an ability to pressure the youth into accepting responsibility as well as beginning to gain insight into their own thoughts and actions.[54] Group modalities work best with juvenile sex offenders when individual offenders are confronted and supported by other juvenile offenders. Treatment should focus on the behavior of sexual offending and the causes, social skills, and cognitive processing errors.[55]

Types of Treatment for JSOs

Essentially, there are two types of treatment available for JSOs: residential and community-based. While residential treatment is generally more intensive and usually reserved for serious and chronic sex offenders, a thorough and comprehensive treatment plan by the clinician, which details the youth's history of sexual and nonsexual activity, must be completed. As some experts have noted,

an evaluation of sexual offending and other forms of inappropriate behavior become the guiding source for successful treatment. As
was mentioned, most JSOs can be treated effectively. This is accomplished through establishing appropriate therapeutic goals and
a solid treatment plan.[56]

Residential Treatment

Residential treatments are usually reserved for more serious offenders, but they can have demonstrable impact on changing
youths' behavior. Recent research shows that placing younger
youths with older ones in residential placement may produce lasting effects including a decrease in delinquent behavior, substance
abuse, violence, and adult maladjustment. While often successful, such programs are expensive: some can exceed $100,000 per
juvenile annually.[57] However, according to some experts, there is
no evidence that residential treatment, the more common of the
two types, is more effective than community-based treatment programs.[58]

One example typical of many residential treatment programs
is The Juvenile Sex Offender Program as part of the Psychiatric
Solutions Inc. (PSI). The PSI program is a secure unit that provides
intensive treatment for moderate to high-risk juvenile sex offenders between the ages of 12–18, and has a separate program that
targets younger adults, those 18–20 years of age. Rehabilitation
takes place in a multi-modal treatment facility that provides residents with a comprehensive treatment plan to reintegrate them
back into the community. The average length of stay is 12 to 18
months; however, this varies based on how well clients respond
to treatment.

The PSI program provides intensive treatment services, structure,
and security, which assist in the individual's reintegration into the
larger community. Specific treatment interventions focus on: sexual
aggression, empathy development, healthy relationships, and relapse
prevention. In addition, the program provides courses on anger management and independent living skills. The PSI program targets youths
who have never received sex offense treatment, who have started treat-

ment but have not completed it, or who have completed treatment but continue to require intensive supervision.[59]

Community-Based Treatment

These types of treatment programs are less expensive than residential ones and can offer an effective alternative for less seriously disturbed offenders. Community-based treatment also offers a transitional stage between residential treatment and reentry into the larger community upon release. Examples of community services include marriage and family therapy; life skills and social skills training, which teach youths how to live independently and to effectively interact with others; anger management training; and seminars to improve offenders' impulse control, which is a key component in avoiding relapse sexual behaviors.[60]

According to most experts, community-based or *outpatient* treatment works best in those instances where the sexual offense was the first one for the client, it appears to be an exception to an otherwise law-abiding life, and there is no history of chronic antisocial or violent behavior. It also works best when that offense was a non-violent one, meaning it did not involve the threat of harm, use of physical force, and did not pose any risk of physical abuse or injury to the victim. Outpatient treatment also appears successful when the sexual activity did not involve any bizarre or ritualistic interpersonal acts (e.g. bondage), and there is no evidence of any serious psychopathology or disorder exhibited by the offender. As with all forms and programs, community-based or outpatient treatment is more likely to be successful when the offender acknowledges their offense, accepts responsibility for hurting others, is motivated for treatment, and there is someone available who can supervise their daily activities. Finally, a critical component to the success of outpatient therapy is that there are an adequate number of support services available to the offender in the community.[61]

One of the most important areas of community-based treatment is the emphasis on individualized treatment plans that involve the coordination of community services, participation by family members, as well as delinquency authorities. Collectively this collaboration of effort is sometimes referred to as multi-systemic treatment interventions (MST). What makes MST effective is that it is a comprehensive attempt to deal with the specific sexual behaviors by taking into account the context in which those behaviors exist.[62]

The goal of MST is to empower parents and youths with skills and resources to support positive behavior. For parents, MST interventions include strategies to improve communication between teachers and parents and providing structure for the youth in afterschool activities, particularly those that affect academic success. For youths, interventions include strategies that enhance appropriate friendships and even dating relationships, teaching youths to learn empathy, and identifying the aforementioned "triggers" that led to offending in the first place. The goal, of course, is that by identifying situations and circumstances that create an environment where the person might reoffend, they can better avoid those situations before they become problematic.[63]

Unfortunately, while the MST model appears to have the greatest level of empirical support, only a small number of programs actually employ it as their treatment model: less than 7% according to the Office of Sex Offender Management.

While MST programs are given a great deal of attention, with a heavy emphasis on holistic healing as well as taking into account the many factors that contribute to JSO behavior, some experts contend that integrating restorative justice into the model would greatly enhance its ability to provide effective treatment. Restorative justice, as a philosophy, is the belief that crime harms people and communities and creates the need to reconcile, repair, or restore the harm that occurred between the victim and the offender.[64]

Restorative justice focuses less on punishment but maintains the importance of holding offenders accountable for their actions, to convey the message that delinquent behavior is unacceptable and promote taking responsibility for one's actions. Restorative justice is also based on the idea that victims should be empowered in some way by having decision-making authority on the resolution of the crime. Restorative programs emphasize that victims should be a participant in the process so that their concerns and questions about why the crime occurred can be addressed. The overarching goal of restorative justice then is to breed a sense of compatibility between society, the victim, and the offender. If victims of crime are empowered, offenders accept responsibility for their actions and some type of restoration occurs due to the harm that was caused; the bonds within the community will be strengthened and reoffending is likely to decrease. The end result is a more cohesive, peaceful and harmonious society.[65] How do the elements of this philosophy relate to the treatment of JSOs?

Specifically, authorities on restorative justice note that the MST model is very similar in its rehabilitative approach to restorative justice; however, what is missing from MST are the victims, whose issues are not adequately addressed during treatment. Neighbors and family members other than the JSO's legal guardian or parent are also often excluded from the youth's treatment plan, but they might also be able to assist the JSO in his or her recovery. Also missing from MST programs are the few opportunities, other than accepting responsibility for the sexual behavior, for the youth to make amends for their behavior. Perhaps even more important, MST programs do not provide opportunities for the community, who will eventually have to accept the JSO upon completion of the program, to address their concerns and fears regarding the event. Thus, some experts contend that integrating restorative justice concepts into MST provides an even greater opportunity for recovery.[66]

However, most treatment programs for JSOs endorse cognitive-behavioral approaches or relapse-prevention models. Essentially, cognitive-behavioral models help clients change their behavior by changing their thinking patterns. The focus is less on trying to find out the causes of the person's behavior than on addressing the current thoughts, feelings, and behavior. Cognitive therapy is also focused on providing structured and realistic examples and strategies of how to accomplish a new way of thinking and behaving.[67]

Relapse prevention is a subset of the broader cognitive–behavioral framework. This approach does not "cure" the person or remove the behavior. Rather it is designed to identify a range of risk factors that might serve as "triggers" and increase the likelihood of engaging in inappropriate behavior, as well as to find practical strategies to deal with these events over a long period of time. Thus, relapse prevention is really based on the idea that the key is to find ways to prevent those incidents.[68]

Registry Laws

The issues surrounding JSOs are complicated and the public's concerns about this type of victimization make it difficult to convince policymakers and politicians that treatment for most JSOs is an effective approach to addressing the issue. Instead, JSOs are often characterized as adult offenders. This means funding for treating JSOs, perhaps the most effective way of dealing with them, is minimized in favor of more punitive approaches such as incarceration or other forms of legal sanctions.

One strategy that is currently used to address the issues and risks posed by sex offenders are *registry laws*. These laws require convicted sex offenders to register with the local police so their whereabouts are known. The idea of registry laws began in 1996, when President Clinton signed *Megan's Law*. Megan's Law was named for Megan Kanka, who was killed at the age of 7 by a neighbor and twice-convicted sex offender. Megan's Law was controversial because it required released sex offenders to register with local police. The law also required neighborhoods to be given the identity, criminal record, and address of offenders with a high-risk of reoffending. Depending on the perceived risk, different agencies are alerted. Only law enforcement is notified if the offender is a low-risk; schools and day care centers are notified if the offender presents a moderate risk; and all neighbors are notified if the offender poses a high risk to the community. Registry is now required in all 50 states.[69]

Another law, entitled the *Adam Walsh Child Protection and Safety Act* (signed by President Bush on July 27, 2006), integrates information in state sex offender registry systems so that offenders can't evade detection by moving from state to state. The law also strengthens federal penalties for crimes against children and provides grants to states to help them institutionalize sex offenders who have not changed their behavior and are about to be released from prison. The Adam Walsh Child Protection and Safety Act also created regional Internet Crimes Against Children Task Force programs to provide funding and training to help law enforcement combat crimes involving the Internet. The law also addresses improving the ability of child protective service professionals to investigate child abuse cases and do background checks of adoptive and foster parents.[70]

Finally, *Jessica's Law* was passed in 2005. It requires more thorough tracking of offenders, such as DNA samples, ankle bracelets, and GPS tracking. Jessica's Law was named for nine-year-old Jessica Lunsford, who was abducted from her Florida home by a convicted sex offender, sexually assaulted, and buried alive. By 2007, 33 states had passed some version of Jessica's law.[71]

While such laws may ease the concerns of parents and community residents about the threat of sex offenders, a number of issues are raised by requiring JSOs to participate in registry laws. For example, juveniles have lower recidivism rates than adults, but are usually lumped in with adults under new laws. Should a teenager guilty of statutory rape be punished under the same law as an older man guilty of molesting young children? Also, should JSOs have to register with their communities as sex offenders, and if so, for how long? What impact will this have on offenders' ability to obtain jobs and other opportunities? Requiring JSOs to register "labels" them for life. What are the implications of this type of strategy in terms of the labeling effect or even a self-fulfilling prophecy? Nearly all current policies are designed to apply to a large number of sexual offenders, including adult sexual offenders. Examples include the Adam Walsh Child Protection and Safety Act and PROTECT Act of 2003.[72]

The original policies that required registration did not include youths adjudicated as minors, though each state had the option to require such registration. Recently, the Adam Walsh Child Protection and Safety Act of 2006 extended registration requirements to offenders as young as 14 years old for durations as long as 15 years,

25 years, and life. This federal requirement is a minimum; some states, such as South Carolina, require that all sex offenders, regardless of age, register for life. A survey showed that judges had significant reservations about requiring juveniles to register.[73] Mandatory registration has consequences for juveniles that include: direct stigmatization, residency restrictions, employment restrictions, notation on driver's licenses, and automatic expulsion from public schools.[74] However, the emphasis on accountability and push to "get tough" on juvenile offenders, a theme discussed throughout this book, results in lawmakers passing legislation in the absence of important empirical evidence that suggests treatment rather than punishment is a more viable option for most JSOs and that such labeling early in life will have lasting consequences for them as adults.

In a fascinating discussion of the legal issues relating to JSOs, including access to information on JSOs, Franklin E. Zimring, a professor of criminal law at the University of California, Berkeley, wrote *An American Travesty: Legal Responses to Adolescent Sexual Offending*.[75] In this book Zimring suggests altering sealed juvenile records, which can hide evidence of sex offending, and instead use something called "time-conditional record sealing." This form of record sealing is based on the idea that when an adolescent with a record of a sex offense commits another act as an adult, law enforcement would be able to access the juvenile's criminal records to make informed judicial decisions. Other experts have suggested a restricted registration system that would allow certain child-centered employers—like camps and schools—to access high-risk juveniles' records for several years to help ensure that those adolescents and young adults do not work with children. As Zimring notes, keeping juveniles off public registries is not just a civil rights issue. "It's also about bringing some kind of rationality into law enforcement," he says, given that including low-risk offenders in these laws adds to police workloads with no proof that it's actually effective.[76] Given the research on the rates of recidivism and juvenile sex offending, where reoffending rates are quite low, Zimring's proposed changes to the process of record keeping are targeted at the most serious types of offenders.[77]

Case Studies in Delinquency
Conclusion about Austin

As part of its zero tolerance policy regarding inappropriate behavior, Austin's school expelled him for possessing a nude photo of his girlfriend. But is this a case of sex offending, poor judgment, or is Austin the actual victim here? While much has been discussed about the problems of zero tolerance policies in schools, this situation has life-long implications for Austin and his future. Is he really a threat to children in his community? If his participation in treatment is not successful, what conclusions might people draw about Austin and sex offenders in general?

Summary

Juvenile sex offenders (JSOs) often evoke terrifying images in the public since it suggests that offenders violently prey upon young victims. Media accounts of the exploitation of children are responsible for a number of myths regarding JSOs, particularly that they are violent offenders, that the problem is widespread, and that most juveniles who commit sex crimes go on to become adult sex offenders. There is also the popular belief that, like their adult counterparts, little can be done to treat JSOs—they are condemned to a life of this type of activity.

While there are juvenile rapists, most juvenile sex offenders are different from these violent delinquents. There is in fact a wide range of activities that fall under the heading of JSO, most of which include non-violent offenses, such as obscene phone calls, voyeurism, exhibitionism, or what are called *non-contact offenses*. The research also suggests that female JSOs are very similar in characteristics to their male counterparts. However, as was mentioned, both male and female JSOs are very different than the adult sex offender population, both in terms of the extent of their behavior, the type of victims they select, and whether or not they are amenable to treatment.

A number of typologies have been created to offer insight into the wide range of activities as well as the motivations for engaging in sex crimes. While some commit them as a result of experimentation, others engage in sex offending due to a host of their own individual issues related to self-esteem and child abuse. Still others, perhaps the smallest segment of the population, commit sex crimes for the power and control over their victims. This is the group that generates the most interest and fear by the public.

While treatment is often successful with JSOs, the research is fairly clear that the type of treatment that works well with this group is multisystem theory (MST). MST has received a great deal of attention by scholars and other experts who support a holistic approach to treatment. This would include not only cognitive/behavioral therapy, but also relapse prevention and other cognitive modalities that help offenders to come to grips with what they did, to accept responsibility for their actions, and to learn techniques and strategies that will identify certain feelings, attitudes, or behaviors that can lead to reoffending.

Still other experts offer insight into the relationship between MST interventions and a restorative justice philosophy. Advocates of restorative justice, for instance, argue that MST programs are not used that often, in large part because of their expense. Additionally, MST programs ignore the victim and the community as resources in helping the individual to overcome his sexual offending. Thus, a merging of MST programs with an emphasis on restorative justice strategies provides the optimal form of treatment for JSOs.

Registry laws, perhaps the most common way to address sex offenders, have increasingly been applied to JSOs as well. However, given their amenability to treatment, and given that the motives and activities of JSOs are different from their adult counterparts, some experts question whether or not making JSOs register as sex offenders, in some cases, permanently, is in line with the philosophy of the juvenile justice system. Others question whether it makes sense at all since it will negate any efforts to effectively treat the offender. For more chronic and serious offenders, particularly those who go on to become adult sex offenders, some experts argue that sealed records of such offenses as juveniles should be available to employers and members of the community. Given the risks this small group of dangerous individuals presents some scholars believe that the risks posed to the community override concerns about individual privacy.

Notes

1. U.S. Department of Justice, Office of Justice Programs, The Center for Sex Offender Management. 2002. *Myths and Facts About Sex Offenders.* Silver Spring, MD.

2. See http://legal-dictionary.thefreedictionary.com/child.

3. See http://legal-dictionary.thefreedictionary.com/juvenile.

4. See http://legal-dictionary.thefreedictionary.com/Children's+ Rights.

5. http://legal-dictionary.thefreedictionary.com/adolescence.

6. See the National Adolescent Perpetrator Network at http://www. kempe.org/napn/.

7. National Center on Sexual Behavior of Youth. 2003. NCSBY Fact Sheet. July. http://www.ncsby.org/pages/publications/CSBP%20Common%20Misconceptions%20vs%20Current%20Findings.pdf. Retrieved February 12, 2009.

8. Ibid.

9. Ibid.

10. Center for Sex Offender Management, 2002.

11. U.S. Department of Justice, Federal Bureau of Investigation. 2009. *Crime in the United States.* Washington, DC: U.S. Government Printing Office http://www2.fbi.gov/ucr/cius2009/offenses/violent_crime/forcible_rape.html.

12. U.S. Department of Justice, Federal Bureau of Investigation. 2000 and 2007. *Crime in the United States.* Washington, DC: U.S. Government Printing Office. http://www.fbi.gov/ucr/cius 2007/index.html and http://www.fbi.gov/ucr/00cius.htm. Retrieved February 10, 2009.

13. See *Crime in the United States,* 2009, http://www2.fbi.gov/ucr/cius2009/data/table_29.html.

14. Hunter, J. and Becker, J. 1998. "Motivators of Adolescent Sex Offenders and Treatment Perspectives," in J. Shaw (ed.), *Sexual Aggression*. Washington, DC: American Psychiatric Press Inc.

15. Lieb, R., Quinsey, V., and Berliner, L. 1998. "Sexual Predators and Social Policy." In M. Tonry (ed.), *Crime and Justice*, 43–114. Chicago: University of Chicago Press. See also The Center for Sex Offender Management 2005.

16. People v. Jackson (Michael) (2005)128 Cal.App.4th 1009.

17. See for instance Terry, K. 2006. *The Nature and Scope of the Problem of Sexual Abuse of Minors by Catholic Priests and Deacons in the United States*. Available at http://www.nccbuscc.org/ ocyp/John-JayReport.pdf.

18. Pedophiles are usually men who can be attracted to either or both sexes. These individuals often think their exploitation of children is somehow helping them; they might, for example, convince themselves that they are contributing to a child's development in some way. See http://www.psychologytoday.com/conditions/pedophilia.html for more information.

19. National Center on Sexual Behavior of Youth, 2003. *What Research Shows About Adolescent Offenders*. http://www.ncsby.org/pages/publications/What%20Research%20Shows%20About%20Adolescent%20Sex%20Offenders%20060404.pdf (accessed August 9, 2008). See also Ryan, G., Miyoshi, T.J ., Metzner, J. L., Krugman, R. D., and Fryer, G. E. (1996). "Trends in a national sample of sexually abusive youths." *Journal of the American Academy of Child and Adolescent Psychiatry*, vol. 35, No. 1: 17–25.

20. See for example, Worling, J. R. & Curwen, T., (2000). "Adolescent Sexual Offender Recidivism: Success of Specialized Treatment and Implications for Risk Prediction." *Child Abuse and Neglect*, 24(7), 965–982.

21. National Center on Sexual Behavior of Youth 2003; and Katrina Baum, 2005. Juvenile Victimization and Offending, 1993–2003, Washington, DC: Bureau of Justice Statistics. http://www.ojp. usdoj.gov/bjs/pub/ pdf/jvo03.pdf (accessed August 9, 2008).

22. Snyder, H. 2000. *Sexual Assault of Young Children as Reported to Law Enforcement: Victim, Incident, and Offender Charac-*

teristics Washington DC: Department of Justice, Bureau of Justice Statistics. http://www.ojp.usdoj.gov/bjs/pub/pdf/saycrle.pdf (accessed August 10, 2008).

23. Ibid.

24. Ibid.

25. Ibid.

26. Glen E. Davis and Harold Leitenberg, "Adolescent Sex Offenders, 101," *Psychology Bulletin* (1987), 417–419.

27. Donna Vandiver, "A Prospective Analysis of Juvenile Male Sex Offenders: Characteristics and Recidivism Rates as Adults," *Journal of Interpersonal Violence,* vol.21, no.5 (2006), 673–688.

28. Ibid.

29. Zimring, F. 2007. "The Predictive Power of Juvenile Sex Offending: Evidence from the Second Philadelphia Birth Cohort Study," pp. 13–14 as cited in Human Rights Watch. 2008. *Sexual Violence in the U.S.* http://www.hrw.org/reports/2007/us0907/4.htm.

30. Ibid.

31. Ibid.

32. Zimring, F., and Piquero, A. 2007. "Juvenile and Adult Sex Offending in Racine, Wisconsin," January 23, 2007. as cited in Human Rights Watch. 2008. *Sexual Violence in the U.S.* http://www.hrw.org/reports/ 2007/us0907/4.htm.

33. Bauman, S. 2002. "Types of Juvenile Sex Offenders." The Prevention Researcher 9(4): 11–13.

34. Ibid.

35. For a good discussion of the research studies on this as well as news accounts of teachers sleeping with students, see http://www.wnd.com/news/ article.asp?ARTICLE_ID=49389.

36. U.S. Department of Justice, Office of Justice Programs, Center for Sex Offender Management. 2007. *Female Sex Offenders.* Washington, DC: U.S. Government Printing Office. http://www.csom.org/pubs/pubs.html#female_sex_offenders.

37. Department of Justice, 2009. *Crime in the United States, Table 42.* Available at http://www2.fbi.gov/ucr/cius2009/data/table _42.html.

38. Snyder, H., & Sickmund, M. 2006. *Juvenile offenders and victims: 2006 national report.* Washington, DC: U.S. Department of

Justice, Office of Justice Programs, Office of Juvenile Justice and Delinquency Prevention.

39. Ibid.

40. Bureau of Justice Statistics. (2006). *Crime and Victim Statistics.* Washington, DC: U.S. Department of Justice, Office of Justice Programs, Bureau of Justice Statistics http://www.ojp.us doj.gov/bjs/cvict.htm accessed August 10, 2008.

41. Bumby, N. H., & Bumby, K. M. 2004. "Bridging the Gender Gap: Addressing Juvenile Females who Commit Sexual Offences." In O'Reilly, G., Marshall,W. L., Carr, A., & Beckett, R. C. (eds.), *The Handbook of Clinical Intervention with Young People Who Sexually Abuse* (pp. 369–381). New York, New York: Brunner-Routledge.; Frey, L. L. 2006. "Girls Don't Do That, Do They? Adolescent Females Who Sexually Abuse" In R. E. Longo & D. S. Prescott (eds.), *Current Perspectives: Working With Sexually Aggressive Youth and Youth With Sexual Behavior Problems* (pp. 255–272). Holyoke, MA: NEARI Press.; Glaze, L., & Bonczar, T. 2006. *Probation and Parole in the United States, 2005.* Washington, DC: U.S. Department of Justice, Office of Justice Programs, Bureau of Justice Statistics.; Harrison, P. M., & Beck, A. J. 2005. *Prison and Jail Inmates at Midyear 2004.* Washington, DC: U.S. Department of Justice, Office of Justice Programs, Bureau of Justice Statistics; Robinson, S. 2001. "Adolescent Females with Sexual Behavioral Problems: What Constitutes Best Practice?" In Longo, R. E. & Prescott, D. S. (eds.), *Current Perspectives: Working with Sexually Aggressive Youth and Youth with Sexual Behavior Problems* (pp. 273–324). Holyoke, MA: NEARI Press.; Vandiver, D. 2006. "Female Sex Offenders: A Comparison of Solo Offenders and Co-offenders." *Violence and Victims, 21,* 339–354.

42. Mathews, R., Hunter, J. A., & Vuz, J. 1997. "Juvenile Female Sexual Offenders: Clinical Characteristics and Treatment Issues." *Sexual Abuse: A Journal of Research and Treatment, 9,* 187–199.

43. Denov, M., & Cortoni, F. 2006. "Women Who Sexually Abuse Children." In Hilarski, C. & Wodarski, J. S. (eds.), *Comprehensive Mental Health Practice With Sex Offenders and Their Families* (pp. 71–99). Binghamton, NY: The Haworth Press.; Nathan, P., & Ward, T. 2002. "Female Sex Offenders: Clinical and Demographic Features." *The Journal of Sexual Aggression, 8,* 5–21.

44. Vandiver 2006.

45. Office of Sex Offender Management 2007.

46. Zimring and Piquero 2007.

47. See for instance Chaffin, M. and Bonner, B. 1998. "'Don't Shoot, We're Your Children': Have We Gone Too Far in Our Response to Adolescent Sexual Abusers and Children with Sexual Behavior Problems?" *Child Maltreatment*, 3(4): 314–316.

48. Association for the Treatment of Sexual Abusers. 2000. "Position Statement: The Effective Legal Management of Juvenile Sexual Offenders," www.atsa.com/ppjuvenile.html accessed August 10, 2008.

49. Gordon, B. and Schroeder, C.S. 1995. *Sexuality: A Developmental Approach to Problems.* New York: Plenum Press.

50. Jones, M. 2007. "The Case for the Juvenile Sex Offender." *New York Times Magazine* July 21. http://thinkoutsidethecage2.blogspot.com/2007/07/ny-times-case-for-juvenile-sex-offender.html retrieved February 10, 2009.

51. Ibid.

52. Lakey, J. 1994. "The Profile and Treatment of Male Adolescent Sex Offenders." *Adolescence.*

53. Ibid.

54. Ibid.

55. Hunter, J. A., Gilbertson, S. A., Vedros, D., & Morton, M. (2004). "Strengthening Community-based Programming for Juvenile Sex Offenders: Key Concepts and Paradigm Shifts." *Child Maltreatment, 9,* 177–193.

56. Ibid.

57. Ibid.

58. Letourneau, E. J., Bandyopadhyay, D., Sinha, D., & Armstrong, K. (2009). "Effects of Sex Offender Registration Policies on Juvenile Justice Decision Making." *Sexual Abuse: A Journal of Research and Treatment,* 140–157.

59. See PSI. Residential Treatment for Juvenile Sex Offenders. http://www.psysolutions.com/facilities/benchmark/residential.html retrieved February 19, 2009.

60. Ibid.

61. Groth, A. N., Hobson, W. F., Lucey, K. P., St. Pierre, J., & Groth, A. N. (1981). "Juvenile sex offenders: Guidelines for treat-

ment." *International Journal of Offender Therapy and Comparative Criminology, 25,* 265–274.

62. See Koss, M. P., Bahcar, K., and Hopkins, C. Q. 2006. "Disposition and Treatment of Juvenile Sex Offenders from the Perspective of Restorative Justice." In Barabaree, H. E. and Marshall, W. L. (eds.) *The Juvenile Sex Offender.* New York: The Guilford Press, pp.336–357.

63. Ibid.

64. Ibid.

65. Ibid.

66. Ibid.

67. U.S. Department of Justice, Office of Justice Programs, Center for Sex Offender Management. *The Effective Management of Juvenile Sex Offenders in the Community: A Training Manual.* http://www.csom.org/train/juvenile/2/outline.htm retrieved February 19, 2009.

68. Ibid.

69. See http://www.klaaskids.org/pg-legmeg.htm.

70. See http://juvienation.wordpress.com/2008/01/25/states-consider-costs-benefits-on-adam-walsh-act/.

71. See http://www.jmlfoundation.org/StatesJMLLaw.htm.

72. Anderson, A. L. & Sample, L. L. (2008). " Public Awareness and Action Resulting from Sex Offender Community Notification Laws." *Criminal Justice Policy Review, 19,* 371–398.

73. Letourneau, E. J., Bandyopadhyay, D., Sinha, D., & Armstrong, K. (2009). "Effects of Sex Offender Registration Policies on Juvenile Justice Decision Making." *Sexual Abuse: A Journal of Research and Treatment,* 140–157.

74. See for example Sample, L. L. & Kadleck, C. (2008). "Sex Offender Laws: Legislators' Accounts of the Need for Policy." *Criminal Justice Policy Review, 19,* 40–64. Also, Chaffin, M. (2008). "Our Minds are Made Up Don't Confuse Us With the Facts: Commentary on Policies Concerning Children with Sexual Behavior Problems and Juvenile Sex Offenders." *Child Maltreatment, 13,* 110–119.

75. Zimring, F. E. 2004. *An American Travesty: Legal Responses to Adolescent Sexual Offending.* Chicago: University of Chicago Press.

76. Ibid.
77. Ibid.

Chapter 3

Juvenile Prostitution

Case Studies in Delinquency

Nikki is a pretty fourteen-year-old female from Seattle, Washington. Nikki comes from an abusive and dysfunctional family. Her mother and father divorced when Nikki was eleven and she and her younger brother went to live with their mother. Prior to the divorce, her father physically abused Nikki. Nikki's mother recently began dating a man who made Nikki very uncomfortable—he frequently made sexual comments to Nikki that were inappropriate. Nikki's mother ignored these concerns when Nikki brought them to her attention.

One night, Nikki ran away from home after her mother's boyfriend attempted to sexually assault her. With nowhere to go, she went to a friend's house and spent the night. Nikki spent the next two weeks hanging out downtown with her friends. A few of them introduced her to drugs, where she quickly became addicted to methamphetamine. One of Nikki's friends offered her a way to make money.

She introduced Nikki to Tank, who arranged a "date" between Nikki and an older man. Soon Tank became her "boyfriend" and "manager." Nikki moved out of her friend's house and stayed in an apartment shared with several of Tank's girlfriends. Soon the heavy drug use and lifestyle began to have a physical impact on Nikki, making her less attractive to clients. When she couldn't earn enough money, Tank began beating her and claiming she cost him too much money. Desperate for money, food, and drugs, one night Nikki propositioned an undercover police officer. She was arrested and charged with solicitation.

Questions to Consider:
1. What obligations do Nikki's parents have to report her as a runaway?
2. Are Nikki's friends responsible for the abuse she suffers from Tank?
3. Is arrest and conviction the solution to Nikki's problems?

The study of child or juvenile prostitution has, until recently, only received moderate attention by researchers. However, incidents of child trafficking, particularly from other countries into the United States, have generated considerable interest in the topic. While the terms *child prostitution* and *juvenile prostitution* are sometimes used interchangeably, and while both are exploitative acts against young people, there is an important difference between an adolescent prostitute who makes the somewhat voluntary decision to participate in the sex trade and a child who is forced to engage in sex work or participate in child pornography. Juvenile prostitution has been defined as the exchange of personal sexual interactions performed by a person under the age of 18 in return for a form of payment such as money, drugs, shelter, or food.[1]

The relationship between teenage prostitution and runaway and homeless behavior has also been well documented.[2] The reasons for these connections are fairly obvious: youths who run away or are thrown out of the home often find it difficult to earn money legitimately, particularly if they are minors. As a result, many turn to prostitution as a means of survival. Others become involved in the sex trade due to sexual and physical abuse at home. Still others are motivated by a substance abuse problem, while many young prostitutes have a combination of these issues. The important point is that the decision is not usually a completely voluntary one; often it is the least offensive of a wide assortment of unhealthy alternatives.

Once they are on the street, teenage prostitutes face a host of additional risks from clients, other sex workers, and in some cases, pimps. As we will see, life as a sex worker contains a number of physical, mental, and social dangers.[3] Moreover, the population is a considerably large one: researchers in the United States estimated nearly 300,000 cases of juvenile prostitution in 1999,[4] an estimated 400,000 cases in 2000,[5] and nearly half a million cases in 2008.[6] Unfortunately, statistics on the number of youths who participate in prostitution in the United States are based on only those juveniles who have been arrested and adjudicated for prostitution offenses. This suggests that these numbers are only a fraction of the actual number of cases. A recent study reported that there is a strong tendency for law enforcement officers not to formally charge youths in cases of juvenile prostitution compared to adults, which significantly underestimates the scope of the problem.[7]

As an illustration of this underreporting, consider arrest data from the Uniform Crime reports. In 2009, there were 58,724 arrests for prostitution and commercialized vice. Of those, only about 2% were of individuals under the age of 18. There were 1,208 arrests for individuals under age 18, 164 for those under the age of 15, and a remarkable 13 arrests for prostitution under the age of 10. The age category of 18–21 accounted for 14% of all prostitution arrests (See Table 3-1).

Table 3-1
Uniform Crime Reports Arrests for Prostitution 2009[8]

All Prostitution

Arrests	Under Age 10	Under Age 15	Under Age 18	Ages 18–21
59,724	13	164	1,208	8,561

These numbers are in stark contrast to the estimates offered by experts. In a 2004 report by the Office of Juvenile Justice and Delinquency Prevention (OJJDP) on the patterns of juvenile prostitutes, it was clear that the nature of prostitution is changing.[9] While much attention is given to female prostitutes, especially juveniles, who are often treated more as victims by police officers than as offenders, males are increasingly becoming a part of the statistical landscape.

The research also shows that there are many different types of prostitutes, with some choosing to work as independent operators, others in informal groups, while still others are exploited by pimps. The OJJDP report documents that juvenile prostitution generally appears to be an activity that occurs with a single operator and is most likely to occur in homes or other private locations, making it more difficult to study.[10] This is in contrast to the more public nature of adult prostitution, which can occur in cars, streets, alleys, and other more visible areas.

Juvenile Female Prostitution

There are a number of misconceptions about prostitution as it relates to young females. For instance, one myth justifies prostitution by asserting it is a victimless crime.[11] After all, the argument goes, if two consenting adults enter into a transaction to exchange sex for money, where is the harm? While this might be a more compelling argument for adults, which is debatable, when children or juveniles are involved, the harm is more evident. When an adult client participates in a sexual act with a juvenile prostitute, that adult has committed an act of sexual abuse of a child. Similarly, as a general rule, when an adult forces a youth to commit a sex act (such as the case involving a pimp), child sexual abuse, rape, and/or battery, has occurred, which is a felony in many states.[12]

Another myth surrounding juvenile female prostitution is that the individual youth has made a voluntary decision to engage in prostitution. A popular image of juvenile female prostitutes is that they are independent entrepreneurs who maintain control over their lives and finances by selectively engaging in the sex trade. Such an image also suggests a glamorous lifestyle, particularly for "high priced" call girls.[13] In reality, many prostitutes are under the control of a pimp, who takes most of the money they earn. Similarly, in those instances where a young prostitute works in a brothel, a significant percentage of the money is given to "the house." In these types of situations, prostitutes' lives are restricted in many ways to ensure their dependency on the pimp, madam, or the house, in a form of indentured servitude.[14]

Still another myth involves the control of clients. A popular image of young female prostitutes is that they dominate their clients and are fully in control of their encounters with them. However, as much of the research on this subject shows, pimps and clients often victimize juvenile female prostitutes in a variety of ways.[15]

A Profile of Juvenile Female Prostitutes

The secretive and illegal nature of prostitution makes any type of firm description of this population difficult to accomplish. What is known empirically is based on qualitative studies of juvenile female prostitutes, which typically use smaller sample sizes and do not attempt to generalize to the entire population. The collection of such studies, along with official data, allows for broad commentary on the characteristics of this population, such as age, race, family background, and factors that influence their decision to engage in prostitution.[16]

Age

According to the Uniform Crime Reports in 2009, there were a total of 39,437 arrests of females for prostitution, of which 936 were under the age of 18. As Table 3-2 shows, of those, about 40% (367) consisted of offenders age 17, while 24% (220) were age 16, and 19% (175) were age 15. As was mentioned, such data should be interpreted with caution as it reflects those instances where police officers made an arrest for this offense rather than attempting to handle the matter informally or charging a youth with another offense. Many studies suggest that although determining an average age is difficult, the most common ages for female prostitutes are 14–17 years old.[17]

Table 3-2[18]
Uniform Crime Reports
Female Arrests for Prostitution by Age under 18

Age	<10	10–12	13–14	15	16	17
	0.2%	0.1%	8.4%	18.6%	23.5%	39.2%
	(2)	(1)	(79)	(175)	(220)	(367)

Total under age 18: 936
Total Prostitution Arrests: 38,593

Race

According to official statistics, a large percentage of African-American females were arrested for prostitution in 2009. However, this differs from what other researchers have found in their studies of the population, where the overwhelming majority of sex workers are Caucasian.[19] It may be that a shift has occurred, where more African-American females are becoming involved in prostitution, or it is also possible that the differences may be due to a focus by the police on females in general and African-Americans in particular. Other researchers have documented this disproportionality of African-Americans in the criminal justice system.[20]

Table 3-3[21]
Uniform Crime Reports
Female Prostitution Arrests by Race under 18

Race	Percentage
White	39.7% (426)
Black	58.4% (629)
American Indian/Alaska Native	0.4% (4)
Asian or Pacific Islander	1.5% (16)

Total under age 18: 1,072
Total Prostitution Arrests: 38,593

Entrance into Prostitution

There are a variety of factors that contribute to young girls becoming involved in prostitution and remaining in the sex trade. The psychological effects of physical and sexual abuse often result in an increased sense of vulnerability, as well as a sense of isolation, betrayal, and alienation. Early research suggested that there were several factors that played a role in a young female's risk for entry into prostitution. These factors included coming from low socioeconomic status families,[22] exposure to and victimization from domestic violence,[23] chaotic and ineffective parenting,[24] engagement in early sexual experiences,[25] and experiences of sexual abuse.[26] More recent research suggests similar trends, where the most common risk factor for a youth's decision to participate in prostitution relates to family dysfunction, which includes violence, mental illness, and a history of physical and sexual abuse.[27]

Runaway Behavior

Runaway behavior among youths has also been found to be a primary risk factor for entry into prostitution.[28] According to the National Runaway Switchboard, runaway youths typically begin with panhandling as a survival strategy but inevitably turn to the underground and illegal economy, such as prostitution, pornography, shoplifting, and other crimes to make money.[29]

According to some experts, many homeless and runaway youths engage in a host of criminal activities to survive, including trading sex for food, shelter, money or drugs. However, survival sex is usually reserved as a last resort and often serves as an indicator of the sense of desperation many homeless youths feel.[30] Although relatively little is known about the actual circumstances surrounding survival sex, some studies have indicated that it tends to occur with approximately 20% of homeless youths.[31] Not surprisingly, street youths are more likely to trade sex for survival items than teens living in shelters. Additionally, males are more likely to trade sex for money while females are more likely to exchange it for alcohol or drugs.[32]

While some young women voluntarily engage in survival sex, particularly those that have been on the street and have friends who engage in prostitution, some are coerced into it. Some youths, for example, are exploited by an adult who initially provided them with food, shelter, clothing, and other items, only to later demand payment in the form of sex.[33] Others were "turned out" by their boyfriends, who are then paid by clients.[34] Some anecdotal evidence suggests that often times, the girlfriend gets nothing from the transaction.[35]

The Influence of Friends, Relatives, and Other Prostitutes

Entry into prostitution often comes as a result of the influence of friends, who provide opportunities and introductions to clients as well as insight into the nature of the sex trade. Such friends run the spectrum of classmates, childhood friends, or new acquaintances made as a result of living on the street. Other times, family members introduce young girls into prostitution, although there is less evidence that this is a common practice.[36] Sometimes prostitutes work for a pimp as a recruiter and encourage young girls to become involved in prostitution.

Dorothy Bracey, in her classic studies of juvenile prostitution, suggests that using other prostitutes to recruit young women provides benefits to both the recruiter (who is often paid in some way by the pimp for bringing in young girls) and the pimp. For the pimp, this indirect method creates an effective screening mechanism: the experienced prostitute only provides the pimp with girls that have the necessary qualities and characteristics that would make them "good earners." Such a strategy also allows the pimp to use multiple prostitutes to serve as recruiters, thereby allowing the stable of young sex workers to grow more quickly. Moreover, experienced prostitutes provide young girls with companionship that differs from the romantic relationship usually required from a pimp. Interestingly, much of the information on this topic has remained understudied since the 1980s.[37]

The Influence of Pimps and Juvenile Female Prostitution

The relationship between female prostitution and pimps is a complicated one. The physical and psychological dependency that pimps create in the women who work for them can be intense and lasting—somewhere in the young woman's need to feel loved is an unhealthy emotional dependency on her pimp, who then demands that she engage in prostitution as a demonstration of that love and commitment.

Pimps often use a number of techniques to recruit young girls into the sex trade. These include the pretense of love, threats of indebtedness, drug addiction, manipulation, and violence. Similar to the psychological effects of battered women, most juvenile prostitutes who have come under the influence of a pimp continue to work for him even after experiencing the exploitation and violence.[38] One technique used by pimps to create this type of emotional dependence on young women is to give them lavish gifts at the start of their relationship. This is designed to prey upon their emotional vulnerability, particularly those who have experienced abuse, are socially isolated, or have a lack of attachment to others. Juveniles, particularly those who have run away from an abusive home, are ideal candidates for this type of treatment.[39]

A variation on this theme is for some pimps to employ other prostitutes to befriend the victim and to have them provide the initial gifts as a token of friendship. For other pimps, a more direct and violent approach is used. This is particularly useful for youths that are new to the street. This technique can include threats, beatings, or even kidnapping them.[40]

Interestingly, most juveniles do not believe their pimp exploits them. In fact, because the pimp is cast into the role of benefactor/boyfriend, the young woman has a difficult time even acknowledging that he is a pimp. Obviously, the extent of control of the pimp on the juvenile is a function of the girl's perceived need for care and protection, regardless of the pimp's actual behavior.[41]

Substance Abuse and Juvenile Female Prostitution

Substance use has been associated with prostitution by a number of researchers.[42] As exhibited by these studies, the relationship between drug use and involvement in prostitution is a complex one— on one hand the frequent use of drugs may increase the risk of initiation into prostitution. This is supported by the majority of older studies, which suggested that drug and alcohol use appeared before involvement in prostitution. The implication, of course, is that the use of drugs led to prostitution.[43] The rationale behind this is rather simple: the financial constraints created by an addiction can lead users to participate in sex work because it is a way to earn cash quickly.[44] For example, one study found that 66% of prostitutes reported they had used drugs prior to entering into prostitution.[45]

On the other hand, some experts contend that substance use serves not as a motivating factor in the decision to engage in prostitution, but as a consequence of it.[46] Thus, while few researchers argue that there is some type of relationship between drugs and prostitution, they differ in the order in which it affects youths' decisions to become involved in the sex trade.

Physical and Mental Health and Juvenile Female Prostitution

In part because of the nature of the risk-taking behavior and in part because of the physical and psychological stressors that come from living on the streets, such as multiple partners, drug abuse, alcoholism, poor nutrition, and minimal healthcare, many juvenile female prostitutes have extensive health problems, including heart disease, chronic liver disease, sexually transmitted diseases, HIV exposure, and an assortment of other problems.[47]

The relationship between prostitution and mental illness has also been well documented.[48] The stressors related to working in the sex industry create a host of risk factors for prostitutes, including post-traumatic stress disorder (PTSD). This is a psychological reaction to extremely stressful events more commonly associated with war veterans or people who have been involved in serious accidents. Symptoms include depression, anxiety, irritability, insomnia, flashbacks, and nightmares.[49]

In one study, researchers interviewed 475 prostitutes in five countries—the United States, South Africa, Thailand, Turkey, and Zambia—and found that 62% reported being raped, 73% said they had been assaulted, and 68% said they had been threatened with a weapon. The main finding of the study was that the intensity of PTSD experienced by prostitutes was comparable to the level experienced by Vietnam veterans.[50] While this study focused primarily on street-level sex workers, the findings also showed that while there was more physical violence on the street compared to other forms of prostitution, there were no differences in the levels or incidence of PTSD.[51]

To cope with the stressors and challenges related to working in the sex trade, many women develop strategies to justify and minimize their exposure to trauma and exploitation by creating the illusion of control, choice, and purpose. This means that females often attempt to establish rules of what sexual behavior will or will not be tolerated. Realistically, however, the amount the client is willing to pay as well as the influence of the pimp determines the nature of the activity, despite the belief by the prostitute that they are in control of the transaction. Such helplessness and lack of control only exacerbates the psychological trauma these young women experience.

Types of Prostitution

There are a wide range of activities that juvenile female prostitutes engage in and the location, type of client, and price, influence the different categories that can be created to understand female prostitution. While no single typology exists, and while prostitution can occur in a variety of locations, generally speaking the following includes some of the most common locations and activities.

Streetwalkers

Streetwalkers are prostitutes who make themselves available in public and solicit customers who pass by. The services provided include a wide range of activities and most transactions are carried out in public spaces: the client's vehicle, alleys, doorways, public parks, or even in hotels that rent by the hour. According to some experts, most sex acts by prostitutes involve oral sex, usually in the client's vehicle, and the duration is approximately fifteen minutes. While the fee structure can vary widely, a typical fee is approximately $20.[52] Streetwalkers have the least control over the nature of their activities, essentially taking whatever they can get. They are at great physical risk from clients, and because they are so visible, they are the most likely to be arrested.[53]

Hotel Prostitutes

A more upscale female prostitute, the hotel prostitute takes advantage of locations where large numbers of people congregate for relatively short periods of time, such as conventions, conferences, and national sales meetings, which typically convene in large hotels. Hotel prostitutes often spend time in lobbies or hotel bars and solicit clients who patronize these establishments. They also make use of desk clerks, concierges, managers, or other hotel staff who refer clients or simply ignore their presence in the hotel or bar in return for a fee. Because this is a more affluent client base, requiring a more sophisticated type of sex worker, the fees generated are higher than streetwalkers, but there are additional expenses as well.[54]

Escort Services and Call Girls

Some prostitutes are not restricted to a specific location like a particular bar or hotel. Instead, they operate on what is known as an "outcall basis," meaning they are contacted by clients or a referral service that arranges the transaction. These "calls" typically involve affluent clients who want to keep a low profile and avoid the risk of arrest. Customers are typically assigned to prostitutes by the escort agency, which charges a fee to the customer. The prostitute then negotiates the price for specific services with the customer. The fees earned by this type of prostitute are exceptionally high, in part because of the nature of the clientele and in part because of the high level of discretion offered to customers. It also requires a higher level of sophistication by sex workers.[55]

House or Brothel Prostitutes

While illegal brothels exist in many cities around the country, the only state that has legalized prostitution is Nevada. However, even in this state there are a number of restrictions placed on the sex trade, one of which is that prostitution cannot occur within city limits. This means legal brothels are only found in rural locations, all of which operate at the discretion of the individual county.[56]

Prostitutes typically are women (although in 2008 males were granted the right to operate in brothels)[57] who are brought in on a contract basis and reside on site for a period of time. Sex workers in these establishments are expected to spend considerable amounts of time in the lounge areas and to be available for customers. The client pays the brothel and the prostitute receives his or her fees (typically 40–60% of the revenue generated, minus deductions for room, board, and supplies).[58] Prostitutes working in brothels have little control over their work environment and are also controlled by state and county regulations that require them to be fingerprinted and to undergo frequent medical examinations. However, compared to streetwalkers, the nature of the activity ensures a greater level of safety for the worker from abusive clients.[59]

Exiting Prostitution

Exiting from prostitution is a difficult transition for many women. The long-term effects of the sex trade, as well as life on the street, tends to have an impact on the sex workers' appearance, making them less attractive to clients. As this occurs, prostitutes may resort to more risky behaviors to earn a living, thus placing them in greater physical jeopardy. Others may begin taking steps to leave the business, if such an opportunity presents itself. However, even for these fortunate few, the integration into the "straight life" is not easy. Additionally, the substance abuse problems that played a role in their previous lives make it difficult to sever all the ties connected to the sex trade.[60]

Case Studies in Delinquency
Conclusions about Nikki

Given what you have just read about the way young women become involved in the sex trade, what can we say about Nikki's situation? Is it a relatively common set of circumstances or is her situation rather unique? What do you think will happen as she continues to suffer from the effects of her drug addiction? What are the chances that she will be able to become a productive and healthy adult?

Juvenile Male Prostitution

Historically, male prostitution has taken many forms, including *escort boys*, those who worked in brothels or *kept boys* who served more as a companion to a client than a prostitute.[61] While research on the subject of male prostitutes is still relatively sparse, there have been a few attempts to examine this population. The recent research on juvenile male prostitution also suggests the absence of a pimp or broker to which the youths are psychologically or physically dependent.[62]

Other studies have attempted to identify common characteristics and describe the various motivations for becoming involved in male prostitution.[63] Most of the research in the 1990s focused on the risks of AIDS and on the runaway population. For instance, one group of researchers interviewed 180 male street prostitutes and 180 escort boys in San Francisco and found that almost two-thirds had been tested for HIV. Of those tested, 10% of the street hustlers and almost 25% of the escort boys were HIV positive. Additionally, most of the boys had a high level of understanding about AIDS and HIV, and condom use for anal intercourse was frequent. About half these boys were IV drug users and most had known someone with HIV or AIDS, which could explain the relatively high percentage who were knowledgeable on the disease.[64]

Thus, while there was a growing body of AIDS-related literature on this population during the 1990s, generally speaking, even today little is known about male prostitution. It is referred to colloquially as *hustling,* a term whose meanings can include the activities of confidence men, drug dealers, those who deal with stolen merchandise and, in general, individuals who engage in a variety of illegal activities. However, the label *hustler* is also applied to males who engage in various sexual activities with other males for money, illegal drugs, or some other form of payment. Hustling is incorporated into the definition of prostitution since the person seeks out and attempts to entice as many clients as possible without the benefit of a broker, client list, or other type of intermediary.[65]

Differences and Similarities between Juvenile Male and Female Prostitutes

Juvenile male prostitutes tend to be different in many ways from their female counterparts. Males tend to be older, are more likely to be arrested, and are more likely to be perceived by the police as an offender instead of a victim. As was mentioned, unlike females, male prostitutes tend not to use pimps. It also appears from the official data that juvenile male prostitutes are disproportionately involved in the sex trade. While about 14% of males in general are under the age of 18 in the United States, nearly two-thirds of juvenile prostitutes are males.[66] However, such a finding should be viewed with caution since this figure may be due to greater attention and an increased likelihood of arrest by the police.

Table 3-4[67]
Male Arrests for Prostitution by Age under 18

Age	<10	10–12	13–14	15	16	17
	1.2%	.5.9%	13.6%	12.7%	24.2%	42.1%
	(3)	(14)	(32)	(30)	(57)	(99)

Total Male Arrests under Age 18: 235

While there are significant differences between juvenile male and juvenile female prostitutes, there are also a number of common characteristics. For example, both groups have a long history of sexual, physical, and psychological abuse committed by family members. Additionally, both groups have a history of runaway behavior and their involvement in prostitution was typically the result of the influence of friends who were already involved in the sex trade. Drug use is fairly consistent across both populations as well. Finally, both male and female juvenile prostitutes feel the physical and emotional toll the sex trade exacts on sex workers.[68] Thus, whether they are females or males, there are a host of issues and problems that precipitate involvement in prostitution for males and females, and once they are in the sex trade, it is exceedingly difficult for them to avoid the traps that their adult counterparts experience.

Sexual Orientation and Male Prostitution

A typical discussion of male prostitution inevitably leads to questions about their sexual orientation. Determining one's sexual orientation is difficult largely because people sometimes act in ways that are inconsistent with whom they think they are as individuals. As it relates to sexual behavior, another way of saying this is that erotic feelings for someone do not always constitute a sexual identity. On the other hand, it makes sense to suggest that most people are aware of their preferences for partners and identify themselves in one of three categories: heterosexual, homosexual, or bisexual. However, there are no instruments that definitively measure one's sexual orientation—it is determined largely by the individual's perception of himself or herself. In other words, if they think of themselves as homosexual then that is usually how they are defined.[69]

While measuring sexual orientation is difficult under the best of circumstances, the problems of self-identity are further complicated by age—teenagers are at a time in their lives when there is often confusion and great uncertainty about many things, including who they think they are and what they wish to become. The teenage years are marked by exploration and experimentation, and even in those cases where teens feel certain about their social identities, their cognitive abilities often limit their understanding of the complexity of emotions—in other words, they can easily mistake sexual attraction for affection or conclude that sexual attraction to another person of the same sex means they must be a homosexual.

The media's coverage of homosexuality also sends inconsistent and confusing messages to the public. While much has been made of gay prostitutes in the media, as evidenced by movies such as *My Own Private Idaho*, which characterize male prostitution as an activity primarily committed by homosexuals who would participate in these types of sexual encounters even if they did not get paid for it, the empirical literature suggests otherwise.[70]

Heterosexual Male Prostitutes

Much of the early literature on male prostitution suggested that male prostitutes were actually heterosexual in their orientations. In these studies, male prostitutes conceptualized their activities as part of a larger set of illegal economic opportunities. Considering themselves "hustlers," which includes a number of quasi-legal and illegal activities, prostitution is one of many ways young men earn a living on the street.[71] In one of the most famous studies of juvenile male prostitution, sociologist Albert J. Reiss Jr. found that hustlers did not perceive themselves as homosexual despite the fact that they engaged in some types of homosexual activity.

By limiting the scope of their activities (e.g. no displays of affection to clients and controlling the types of sexual acts performed), as well as by proclaiming a lack of enjoyment in the process (hustlers referred to it as "working" instead of sex), the subjects in Reiss's study could maintain a strong heterosexual identity. In fact, Reiss discovered that some of the boys did not think of themselves as either prostitutes or as homosexuals. Instead, they were hustlers who earned a living in a variety of ways.[72]

As was mentioned, in the 1990s some researchers became interested in the population largely due to the interest in risk behavior and HIV/AIDS issues. Most of the studies during that period focused on knowledge of the disease and preventive steps young prostitutes used to avoid infection with the HIV virus. Many of these research projects involved participants completing a survey and submitting a blood sample to determine their HIV status.

However, in one of the few in-depth ethnographic studies of male prostitutes in New York City, sociologist Robert McNamara examined the lives of 35 male prostitutes in an effort to understand the nature of male prostitution and the issues for many involved in the sex trade. He found that not only did a community of hustlers exist in the Times Square section of New York City, but also there were a number of cultural constraints that placed many of the boys at risk for arrest, injury, or infection with the HIV virus.[73]

For instance, in his interviews with the hustlers, McNamara discovered that while most knew how to define HIV/AIDS and could explain effective means of preventing infection, most used flawed means to prevent it from occurring. The explanation for this inconsistency is found in the cultural values of the hustling community. That is, the need to belong to the community of hustlers was so powerful that hustlers would use what they knew to be ineffective prevention methods (e.g. frequent testing or only seeking out healthy-looking clients) largely because that was the standard screening practice within the group.[74]

Another fascinating discovery was the way most of the hustlers in Times Square identified their sexual orientation—the vast majority considered themselves to be heterosexual. The hustlers of Times Square coexisted with homosexual hustlers, who frequented Times Square and Greenwich Village in order to find clients. As was discovered by Reiss in his study, the hustlers of Times Square distinguished themselves from gay hustlers by limiting the range and scope of activities they would engage in with clients.

Since gay hustlers would perform virtually any sex act with a client if the price were right, heterosexual hustlers were able to maintain their masculine orientation by refusing to engage in such tactics. Additionally, since gay hustlers also enjoyed homosexual activity (and got paid too) heterosexual hustlers did not view their acts as pleasurable. Instead they viewed their participation in prostitution as "working" or "hustling," where they tried to elicit money from clients for as little sex as possible. In this way, the hustlers of Times Square could retain their heterosexual identities.[75]

Homosexual Male Prostitutes

As was mentioned, while some research suggests that homosexual hustlers generally engage in a wider range of sexual activities and derive pleasure from the activity, other experts question the clearly defined lines between homosexual and heterosexual prostitutes.[76] They argue that the stigma attached to a homosexual orientation and the need to present oneself as strong and aggressive, particularly on the street, may cause many homosexual hustlers to project a heterosexual image.[77] Other researchers point out that the tendency for many hustlers to eventually become clients suggests that there is an implied homosexual orientation for most male prostitutes. In short, these experts contend that the attitudes presented by heterosexual hustlers, that prostitution is a simple economic exchange, is not a valid indicator of one's sexual orientation.[78]

More recently, the study of male prostitution has centered on the changing nature of societal perceptions of sex work in general and prostitution by males in particular. In one study, the absence of a strong negative reaction to prostitutes who advertise their services in magazines and on websites is indicative of the declining public stigma about prostitution. This lack of stigma is taken as evidence that society's norms regarding sexual activity in general and sex work in particular have been relaxed. This is especially true for homosexual prostitutes, who are sometimes referred to as *Rent Boys*. Ads placed on the Internet, in gay men's magazines, and social network sites like Craigslist, among other locations, have become popular and more socially acceptable.[79]

The International Trafficking of Children

The study of juvenile and child prostitution has gained greater notoriety due in large part to media stories of the international trafficking of children. While most of these cases involve the importation of children from third world countries, an increasing number involve American children being trafficked to other countries. Within the United States the problem usually involves immigrant children from other countries such as Mexico, Thailand, and Guatemala who are brought into this country for prostitution. In fact, so much attention has been given to the issue of human trafficking that Congress passed the Victims of Trafficking and Violence Protection Act in 2000 and again in 2005. The act defines human trafficking as a commercial sex act induced by force, fraud, or coercion or in which the person influenced to perform such acts is a juvenile.[80]

According to the U.S. Department of Health and Human Services, trafficking in human beings is a modern-day form of slavery, something former President George W. Bush called "a brutal crime that steals innocence and destroys lives."[81] Many victims of human trafficking are forced to work in the sex industry, but trafficking also occurs in various forms of labor exploitation, such as domestic servitude, restaurant work, janitorial work, sweatshop factory work, and migrant agricultural work.[82]

While it is difficult to know the exact numbers, largely because much of this activity is covert in nature and a great deal of it goes unreported, according to the U.S. Department of State, about 1 million children per year are exploited by the global commercial sex trade.[83] Approximately 600,000 to 800,000 men, women, and children annually are trafficked across international borders worldwide, and an estimated 14,500 to 17,500 of those victims are trafficked into the United States. According to the International Labor Organization (ILO), a United Nations Agency, millions more are trafficked within their own countries.[84]

According to another U.S. Department of State report, about 70% of the female victims who are trafficked are forced into the commercial sex trade while the remainder consists of victims of forced labor.[85] Obviously the primary reason for such a widespread problem is money: the yearly profits from the human trafficking industry have been estimated to be approximately $32 billion per year.[86] Additionally, this phenomenon is so widespread that the U.S. Department of Health and Human Services estimates that not only is trafficking of humans the fastest growing criminal industry in the world, it remains tied with arms dealing as the second largest criminal enterprise, after drug dealing.

Traffickers use various techniques to instill fear in victims and to keep them enslaved. While some traffickers literally keep their victims under lock and key, the more frequent practice is to use less obvious techniques, including the following:

- **Debt bondage.** This is a modern-day version of indentured servitude, where the victim must pay off an exorbitant debt before they are free to leave.
- **Isolation from friends, family, and the general public.** This is accomplished by limiting contact with outsiders and making sure that any contact is monitored or superficial in nature.
- **Confiscation of passports, visas and/or identification documents.** This results in preventing victims from fleeing their captors.
- **Threats or use of violence against family members.**
- **Threats of shaming victims by exposing their activities to family members.**
- **Telling victims they will be imprisoned or deported for immigration violations if they contact authorities.**
- **Control of victims' money by stating they are holding it for them.** This is a common technique used by pimps on female prostitutes.[87]

Summary

While the issues stemming from juvenile prostitution are reflected in the policies and programs implemented to help this segment of the population, there are actually few resources available to deal with prostitution in particular. While some communities have programs to help runaway and homeless youths, such as shelters, counseling services, and other forms of aid to meet basic needs, programs to help them avoid sex work are rare.

Because the problem of juvenile prostitution is related to poverty, running away, family discord, and other issues, it is im-

portant to identify and understand the context of delinquent behaviors since they may provide insight into the nature of the problem. In fact, one might argue that delinquent behaviors like
prostitution are actually symptomatic of a larger set of structural
problems.

While the issue remains a complex one, the solutions to addressing the problem of juvenile prostitution is found in noting
why such behavior is occurring rather than simply trying to minimize its effects through arrest and other formal mechanisms. Such
an approach allows for a more comprehensive understanding of
the problem, which will result in developing strategies and solutions that will be more effective in the long run. In the case of juvenile prostitution, as well as juvenile sex offending, the real
problems relate to family issues, such as abuse, neglect, and running away.

In 2008, an interesting twist emerged in the study of juvenile
prostitution, which also potentially impacts decisions relating to
public policy. Male prostitutes, who have historically been less visible and virtually ignored in the empirical literature, gained the national spotlight when the state of Nevada allowed male prostitutes
to legally operate. In the past, what prevented male prostitutes from
legally participating in the sex trade was a legal technicality that
mandated cervical exams for sex workers who legally operated in
the state. When this requirement was lifted, male prostitutes were
allowed to operate as legal sex workers. However, the most noted
criticism of the change came from brothel owners, who believe homosexual prostitutes operating in brothels will tarnish the reputa-
tion of the industry in general and brothels in particular.[88]

Notes

1. Hwang, S., & Bedford, O. 2004. "Juveniles' Motivations for
Remaining in Prostitution." *Psychology of Women Quarterly*, 28,
136–146.

2. See for instance, Weisberg, D. K. 1985. *Children of the Night.*
Boston, MA: Lexington Books. See also Nadon, S. M., Koverola,

C., and Schluderman, E. 1998. "Antecedents to Prostitution." *Journal of Interpersonal Violence* 2: 206–221. See also Shaver, F. M. 2005. "Sex Work Research." *Journal of Interpersonal Violence.* 20: 296–319. See Mitchell, K. J.; Finkelhor, D.; and Wolak, J. 2009. "Contemplating Juvenile Prostitution as Child Maltreatment: Findings from the National Juvenile Prostitution Study." *Child Maltreatment,* 15: 18–36. See also Finkelhor, D. and Ormrod, R. 2004. *Prostitution of Juveniles: Patterns from NIBRS.* Washington, DC: Office of Juvenile Justice and Prevention. Available at http://www. ncjrs.gov/pdffiles1/ojjdp/203946.pdf.

3. Mitchell, Finkelhor and Wolak, 2009; Finkelhor and Ormond, 2004.

4. ECPAT, 1999.

5. Ibid.

6. Federal Bureau of Investigation (2005). *Crime in the United States 2000.* Available at http://www.fbi.gov.

7. Finkelhor and Ormond, 2004.

8. U. S. Department of Justice, Federal Bureau of Investigation. 2009. *Crime in the United States. Table 32.* Available at http://www.fbi.gov/about-us/cjis/ucr/crime-in-the-u.s/2009.

9. While the Uniform Crime Reports system collects information on a limited number of index crimes and gathers few details on each crime event (except in the case of homicide), NIBRS collects a wide range of information on victims, offenders, and circumstances for a greater variety of offenses. Offenses include, homicide, assault, rape, robbery, theft, arson, vandalism, fraud, and embezzlement, and a category called crimes against society, which include ,drug offenses, gambling, and prostitution. NIBRS also collects information on multiple victims, multiple offenders, and multiple crimes that may be part of the same episode.

10. Finkelhor and Ormond, 2004.

11. Meier, R. F. and Geis, G. 1997. *Victimless Crime? Prostitution, Drugs, Homosexuality, and Abortion* Los Angeles, CA: Roxbury.

12. While every state determines its own laws, as a general rule, forced sexual behavior with a minor is considered child sexual abuse and is a felony in most states. See http://www.freelaw answer.com.

13. Meier and Geis, 1997.

14. See for instance, Williamson, C. and Cluse-Tolar, T. 2002. "Pimp Controlled Prostitution." *Violence Against Women*, 8(9): 1074–1092.

15. Ibid.

16. See for instance, Weisberg, 1985; Nadon, Koverola, and Schluderman, 1998; Shaver, 2005; Mitchell, Finkelhor, and Wolak, 2009.

17. Ibid.

18. See U.S. Department of Justice, Federal Bureau of Investigation. *Crime in the United States 2009*. Table 40 available at http://www2.fbi.gov/ucr/cius2009/data/table_40.html.

19. Weisberg, 1985.

20. See for instance McNamara, R. H. and Burns, R. 2009. *Multiculturalism in the Criminal Justice System*. New York: McGraw-Hill.

21. Ibid, Table 43. Available at http://www2.fbi.gov/ucr/cius 2009/data/table_43.html.

22. Hwang & Bedford, 2004; Silbert, M. H., & Pines, A. M. 1981. "Sexual Child Abuse as an Antecedent to Prostitution." *Child Abuse and Neglect*, 5, 407–411. See also Silbert, M. H., & Pines, A. M. 1982. "Entrance into Prostitution." *Youth and Society*, 13, 471–500. Silbert, M. H., & Pines, A. M. 1983. "Early Sexual Exploitation as an Influence in Prostitution." *Social Work*, 28, 285–289. Schaffer, B., and DeBlassie, R. R. 1984. "Adolescent Prostitution." *Adolescence*, 19, 689–696.

23. Brown, M. E. 1979. "Teenage Prostitution." *Adolescence*, 14, 665-680. Pedersen, W., & Hegna, K. 2003. "Children and Adolescents Who Sell Sex: A Community Study." *Social Science and Medicine*, 56, 135–147. Seng, M.1989. "Child Sexual Abuse and Adolescent Prostitution; an Analysis." *Adolescence* 24(95): 665–675.

24. Seng,1989; Weisberg, K. 1985. *Children of the Night: A Study of Adolescent Prostitution*. Toronto: Lexington.

25. Bracey, D. H. 1983. "The Juvenile Prostitute: Victim and Offender." *Victimology*, 8, 151–160.

Hwang & Bedford, 2004; James, J., & Meyerding, J. 1978. "Early Sexual Experience as a Factor in Prostitution." *Archives of Sexual Behavior*, 7, 31–42.

26. Brown, 1979; Finkelhor, D. and Ormrod, R. 2004. *Prostitution of Juveniles: Patterns from NBIRS*. Washington, DC: U.S. Government Printing Office. http://www.ncjrs.org/html/ojjdp/

203946/page1.html; Pedersen & Hegna, 2003; Schaffer & DeBlassie, 1984; Seng, 1989.

27. Estes, R. J. and Weiner, N. A. 2001. *The Commercial Sexual Exploitation of Children in the U.S., Canada, and Mexico.* Philadelphia, PA: University of Pennsylvania School of Social Work. Center for the Study of Youth Policy.

28. See for instance, Bracey, 1983; Brown, 1979; Chesney-Lind, M., & Shelden, R. G. 2004. *Girls, Delinquency, and Juvenile Justice* (3rd ed.). Belmont, C.A.: Thomson-Wadsworth. See also Cusick, L. 2002. "Youth Prostitution: A Literature Review." *Child Abuse Review*, 11, 230–251. See Erickson, P. G., Butters, J., McGillicuddy, P., and Hallgren, A. 2000. "Crack and Prostitution: Gender, Myths, and Experiences." *Journal of Drug Issues*, 30, 767–788. Flowers, R. B. 2001. *Runaway Kids and Teenage Prostitution.* Westport, CT: Praeger. See also Hwang & Bedford, 2004; Pedersen & Hegna, 2003; Schaffer and DeBlassie, 1984.

29. See National Runaway Switchboard. http://www.nrscrisisline.org/media/call_stats_thirdparty.html.

30. See Hagan, J. and McCarthy, B. 1997. *Mean Streets: Youth Crime and Homelessness.*

Cambridge, MA: Cambridge University Press. Institute for Children and Poverty.

Halcon, L., & Lifson, A. 2004. "Prevalence and Predictors of Sexual Risks among Homeless Youth Homeless Youth." *Journal of Youth and Adoles*cence, 33(1): 71–80. Hammer, H., Finkelhor, D., & Sedlak, A. 2002. Runaway/thrownaway Children: National Estimates and Characteristics. *National Incidence Studies of Missing, Abducted, Runaway and Thrownaway Children.* Johnson, K. A. 2006. "Trading Sex: Voluntary or Coerced? The Experiences of Homeless Youth." *Journal of Sex Research.* , 43, 208–216.

31. See van Leeuwen, J. M.; Hopfer, C.; Hooks, S.; White, R.; Petersen, J.; and Pirkopf, J. 2004. "Snapshot of Substance Abuse Among Homeless and Runaway Youth in Denver." *Journal of Community Health* 29, 217–229.

32. Tyler, K., Hoyt, D., Whitbeck, L., & Cauce, A. 2001. "The Effects of High-risk Environment on Sexual Victimization of Homeless and Runaway Youth." *Violence and Victims*, 16, 441–455.

33. Hagan and McCarthy, 1997.

34. Tyler et al. , 2000; Hagan and McCarthy, 1997.

35. Johnson, 2006.

36. Weisberg, 1985.

37. See Bracey, D. H. 1979. *Baby-Pros: Preliminary Profiles of Juvenile Prostitutes.* New York: John Jay Press.

38. Ibid.

39. Ibid.

40. Kennedy, M.A.; Klein, C.; Jessica, T. K.; Cooper, B.S.; Yuille, J.C. 2007. "Routes of Recruitment: Pimps' Techniques and Other Circumstances that lead to Street Prostitution." Journal of Aggression, Maltreatment and Trauma 15(2): 1–19.

41. Ibid.

42. Weber, A. E.; Boivin, J.F.; Blais, L.; Haley, N., and Roy, E. (2004). "Predictors of Initiation into Prostitution Among Female Street Youth." *Journal of Urban Health: Bulletin of the New York Academy of Medicine*, 81(4): 584–590.

43. Tyler, K. A., & Johnson, K. A. 2006. "Trading Sex: Voluntary or Coerced? The Experiences of Homeless Youth." *Journal of Sex Research*, 43, 208–216. See also Brown, 1979; Erickson et al., 2000.

44. See Schaffer and DeBlassie, 1984 and Erickson et al., 2000.

45. Shaffer and DeBlassie, 1984.

46. Bour, D. S., Young, J. P., and Henningsen, R. 1984. "A Comparison of Delinquent Prostitutes and Delinquent Non-Prostitutes on Self-concept." *Journal of Offender Counseling, Services, and Rehabilitation*, 9, 89–101. See also Cusick, 2002, Hwang and Bedford, 2004.

47. Sterry, D. H. and Martin, R. J. (eds.). 2009. *Hos, Hookers, Call Girls, and Rent Boys.* New York: Soft Skull Press.

48. Ibid.

49. Farley, M. and Barkan, H. 1998. "Prostitution, Violence Against Women, and Post-Traumatic Stress Disorder." *Women and Health*, 27(3): 37–49.

50. Ibid.

51. Ibid.

52. Levitt, S. A. and Venkatesh, S. A. 2007. "An Empirical Analysis of Street-Level Prostitution." Available at http://economics. uchicago.edu/pdf/Prostitution%205.pdf.

53. http://law.jrank.org/pages/1879/Prostitution-Typology-prostitution.html.

54. Ibid.

55. Ibid.

56. See http://www.lasvegaslogue.com/prostitution.

57. Family Research Council. 2008. "Nevada Welcomes Male Prostitutes, Brothel Owners Not Happy." Opposing Viewpoints. Available at http://www.opposingviews.com/articles/opinion-Nevada-welcomes-male-prostitutes-brothel-owners-not-happy.

58. http://law.jrank.org/pages/1879/Prostitution-Typology-prostitution.html.

59. Ibid.

60. Ibid.

61. Coombs, Neil. 1974. "Male Prostitution: A Psychological View of Behavior." *American Journal of Orthopsychiatry* 44(5): 782–789. See also Drew, Dennis, and Jonathan Drake. 1969. *Boys for Sale.* New York: Brown Book Company. See also Weisberg, 1985.

62. Ibid.

63. See Weisberg 1985; Butts, W. M. 1947. "Boy Prostitutes of the Metropolis." *Journal of Clinical Psychopathology* 8: 673–681. See also Jersild, J. 1956. *Boy Prostitution.*Copenhagen, Denmark: C. E. Gad. Campagna, D. J., and Poffenberger, D. L. 1988. *The Sexual Trafficking of Children.* South Hadley, Mass: Auburn House. James, J. 1982. *Entrance into Male Prostitution.* Washington DC: The National Institute of Mental Health. MacNamara, D. E. J. 1965. "Male Prostitution in American Cities: A Socioeconomic or Pathological Phenomenon?"*American Journal of Orthopsychiatry* 35:204. Luckenbill, D. 1986. "Entering Male Prostitution." *Urban Life* 14(2): 131–53.

64. See Elifson, K., Boles, J., and Sweat, M. 1993. "Risk Factors Associated with HIV Infection Among Male Prostitutes." *American Journal of Public Health* 83: 79–83. See also Calhoun, T. and Pickerill, B. 1988. "Young Male Prostitutes: Their Knowledge of Selected Sexually Transmitted Diseases." *Psychology: A Journal of*

Human Behavior 25(3/4): 1–8. Pleak, R. R., and Meyer-Bahlburg, H. 1990. "Sexual Behavior and AIDS Knowledge of Young Male Prostitutes in Manhattan." *Journal of Sex Research* 27(4): 557–587. Borus-Rotheram, M. and Koopman, C. 1991. "Sexual Risk Behaviors, AIDS Knowledge and Beliefs about AIDS among Runaways." *American Journal of Public Health* 81(2): 206–208.

65. See McNamara, Robert P. 1994. *The Times Square Hustler: Male Prostitution in New York City.* Westport, CT: Praeger.

66. *Statistical Abstract of the United States.* 2009. http://www.census.gov/compendia/statab/2011/tables/11s0007.pdf; *Crime in the United States* 2009. Table 38. Available at http://www2.fbi.gov/ucr/cius2009/data/table_38.html.

67. *Crime in the United States,* 2009. Table 38.

68. See Weisberg, 1985.

69. See West, D. J. and Villier, B. 1993. *Male Prostitution.* New York: Haworth Press.

70. Ibid.

71. See for instance, Coombs, 1974; Butts, 1947; Jersild, 1956; Campagna and Poffenberger, 1988; Luckenbill, 1986; Drew, Dennis and Drake, 1969.

72. Reiss, 1961. A. J. 1961. "The Social Integration of Queers and Peers," *Social Problems* 9(2): 102–20.

73. McNamara, 1994.

74. Ibid.

75. Ibid.

76. Ibid. See also Reiss, 1961.

77. West and Villier, 1994.

78. Benjamin, H. and Masters, R. E. L. 1964. *Prostitution and Morality.* New York: Julian Press.

79. Sterry and Martin, 2009.

80. Finkelhor and Ormrod, 2004.

81. U.S. Department of Health and Human Services. 2006. *HHS Fights to Stem Human Trafficking.* Available at http://www. hhs.gov/news/factsheet/humantrafficking.html.

82. Ibid.

83. U.S. Department of State, *The Facts About Child Sex Tourism*: 2005.

84. U.S. Department of Health and Human Services, 2006.

85. U.S. Department of State, *Trafficking in Persons Report*: 2007.

86. U.S. Department of Justice, *Assessment of U.S. Government Activities to Combat Trafficking in Persons*: 2004.

87. Ibid.

88. Family Research Council, 2008.

Chapter 4

Fire Starters and Juvenile Arson

Case Studies in Delinquency

Steve is a fifteen-year-old runaway who has spent the last year-and-a-half living on the streets of Cheshire, Connecticut. Steve ran away from his parents' home after a juvenile court judge sent him to a residential treatment facility for his tendency to set fires in the woods nearby. The latest incident involved Steve gathering up a pile of leaves in his family's backyard, pouring gasoline on them, and throwing a firecracker into the pile. The fire quickly spread and caused considerable damage to the family's home. A neighbor observed Steve start the fire and immediately contacted the local fire department. Had the fire fighters not arrived quickly, the house would have likely burned to the ground. Fortunately, no one was home at the time.

Steve's family situation is quite dysfunctional: his father physically, emotionally, and verbally abuses his mother as well as Steve and his three younger brothers. This environment has profoundly affected Steve. Normally a good student with a wide circle of friends, in the last year he has withdrawn socially and has become unpredictable in his moods. In fact, Steve often acts violently to those around him without provocation. His behavior in school has also become problematic—he has become defiant to teachers and administrators and has had several fights with schoolmates.

Steve has even been arrested on several occasions for assault and threatening his neighbors, peers, and teachers. During his last visit to juvenile court, a judge ruled that he should be sent to a residential treatment facility. Steve escaped custody and began living on the streets. Last week, a man offered Steve $250 to burn

83

down his abandoned warehouse. Steve was caught and charged with arson.

Questions to Consider:

1. Is the fire setting behavior symptomatic of a larger set of problems or is Steve's fascination with fire related to normal teenage curiosity?
2. Does Steve have serious emotional problems that require professional intervention?
3. Given the trauma of abuse and neglect, is there anything that can be done to help Steve?

Whether it is because of the news media's tendency to cover "sexier" delinquent activities, such as youth violence or drug abuse, or for some other reason, many people overlook the seriousness of juveniles who set fires. This tendency, however, ignores the enormous consequences that come from such activity. In this chapter we will summarize the relevant literature on the nature of juvenile fire setting behaviors, outline common characteristics of juvenile arsonists, and offer insight into the nature of treatment for juvenile fire starters. Interestingly, despite the significant economic and social costs related to juvenile fire starting, the available research on the subject is limited. That is, we simply do not know a lot about this population nor the most effective means of treating this type of behavior.

The Nature of the Problem

According to the Uniform Crime Reports, arson is defined as "any willful or malicious burning or attempting to burn, with or without intent to defraud, a dwelling house, public building, motor vehicle or aircraft, personal property of another, etc."[1] In other words, arson is an intentional act (not an accidental fire) that is started for fun, for revenge, for curiosity's sake, for attention, or for any number of other reasons.

The consequences of arson are expensive, both financially and in the cost to human safety. In 2009 the Federal Bureau of Investigation (FBI) reported 59,962 instances of arson resulting in over $900 million worth of damage.[2] From 2004–2006 intentionally set fires accounted for a yearly average of 375 deaths and 1,300 injuries.[3] These fires pose a special threat to young children and the elderly, who are more susceptible to smoke inhalation and are less capable of escaping on their own.[4] For the purposes of this book, our interest in arson stems from the fact that over the past 15 years roughly half of all arson arrests were children under the age of 18.[5] In fact, in 2009, 15- to 17-year-olds were the most likely offenders, followed by 13- to 14-year-olds. See Table 4-1.

Table 4-1
Juvenile Arrests for Arson by Age 2009[6]

Age	Arrests
<10 years old	218 (5.1%)
11–12 years old	769 (18.2%)
13–14 years old	1,492 (35.3%)
15–17 years old	1,737 (41.2%)
Total Arrests <18	4,216
All Ages:	9,509

Both arrest and clearance rates for arson are high among juvenile offenders. Clearance rates are the number of instances where an arrest is made or a suspect is identified. In 2009 the clearance rate for juvenile arson was roughly 35%, the highest for all clearances involving persons under the age of 18, and the average cost of damage from arson to property was $17,411 (Figure 4-1). Structures were the most frequent target, constituting 44.4% of all fires set, and representing one of the highest clearance rates, particularly community buildings.[7]

In attempting to understand the nature of juvenile arson, previous literature has made an important distinction between *fire play* and *fire setting*. Youths who engage in fire play are simply fascinated with fire—they do not start fires to harm people or property, but rather out of curiosity or reckless play.[9] According to the United States Fire Administration, approximately 40% of all children have engaged in fire play.[10] Although both fire setting and fire play can generate the same result (injury, damage to property, or loss of life), fire setting occurs as a means to achieve some objec-

Figure 4-1
2009 Uniform Crime Reports
Arson by Property Type[8]

Property classification	Number of arson offenses	Percent distribution	Percent not in use	Average damage	Total clearances	Percent of arsons cleared
Total	51,389	100.0		$17,411	9,601	18.7
Total structure:	22,867	44.5	17.1	33,118	5,433	23.8
Single occupancy residential	10,859	21.1	17.6	31,000	2,380	21.9
Other residential	3,629	7.1	13.4	30,442	933	25.7
Storage	1,525	3.0	20.4	29,885	319	20.9
Industrial/ manufacturing	209	0.4	23.9	93,287	51	24.4
Other commercial	2,009	3.9	16.1	78,249	446	22.2
Community/ public	2,481	4.8	16.6	26,313	848	34.2
Other structure	2,155	4.2	19.6	10,512	456	21.2
Total mobile:	14,577	28.4		7,715	1,326	9.1
Motor vehicles	13,846	26.9		7,292	1,203	8.7
Other mobile	731	1.4		15,709	123	16.8
Other	13,945	27.1		1,791	2,842	20.4

tive, such as revenge or to receive attention. This differs from fire play behavior, which is usually episodic and less likely to be repeated.[11] Fortunately, children who engage in fire play are much less likely to repeat the dangerous behavior of their fire setting peers.

It is also important to distinguish the juvenile fire setter from the adult arsonist. While a teenager might understand some of the consequences to starting a fire, society generally does not assign him or her the same level of responsibility as an adult since youths generally lack the ability to grasp the consequences of their behavior.[12] However, chronic juvenile arsonists are different from most youths and this type of offender requires a more complex form of intervention.

Since there are a host of environmental and psychological factors at work, it is essential to offer insight into the nature of fire setting behavior and to provide some type of theoretical framework to explain the nature of this activity.

Sociological Factors to Explain Firestarting

Juvenile fire setting behaviors are the result of a host of interrelated psychological and environmental factors. Despite the complexity of the issue, previous research has established some commonality among offenders. Most are male and many (perhaps as much as 70%) demonstrate poor school performance despite receiving intelligence scores that were equivalent to their peers. Additionally, the research indicates that the majority of children who engage in fire setting have suffered abuse, neglect, or some form of family dysfunction including parental psychosis, domestic violence, parental drug abuse or other criminal behaviors.[13] This link between physical and/or emotional abuse and neglect and fire setting behaviors has been consistently supported for nearly 70 years.[14] More recently, researchers established a relationship between sexual abuse and fire setting. This line of research is not surprising given the known connection between child maltreatment and juvenile delinquency. Indeed, as with other forms of juvenile delinquency, abused children learn poor coping and interaction strategies while repeatedly experiencing stress and anxiety in the home.[15]

What is interesting, however, is that children who are fire setters have suffered more severe levels of family dysfunction than other psychiatric inpatients.[16] This suggests that not only do juvenile fire setters suffer at the hands of their care takers, but the suffering is more severe than other children who have been hospitalized with psychiatric disorders. Given that the most common age for offending is under 14, this pain and trauma was endured during the particularly vulnerable childhood and preadolescent years. Furthermore, while not all juvenile fire setters suffered abuse or neglect, those whose cases are the most severe have experienced maltreatment. Specifically, when compared with non-abused fire setters, maltreated youths are at increased risk for setting multiple fires, for using a variety of ignition methods and targets, and recidivism.[17] These data suggest that children who are engaged in fire setting are experiencing a high level of strain in their homes.

While child maltreatment is a risk factor for fire setting, the presence of abuse or neglect is not enough to explain why a child might turn to that particular form of deviance. Other research demonstrates a mechanism that family instability generates a sense of anxiety and anger in the child while simultaneously limiting his or her opportunities to express those emotions without fear of further abuse. Minus a healthy outlet for these feelings, the child will externalize them by acting out in deviant or aggressive ways.

In a study by Root et al. (2008), child maltreatment was significantly related to a high externalizing score on the child behavior checklist (CBCL), a common measurement tool. Furthermore, a high externalizing score was significantly related to the severity of fire setting behaviors.[18] Put another way, a high score on the CBCL indicates that the respondent is very likely to deal with his or her emotions through externalizing behaviors such as fighting or picking arguments. Children who are abused or neglected by their parents do not have a healthy outlet for their stress and are, therefore, more likely to deal with that strain by acting out. Root's research suggests that child abuse and family dysfunction create a combination of fear, anger, and anxiety in children while simultaneously limiting their ability to express those emotions. When this emotional distress is combined with available ignition sources, a lack of adult supervision, and a poor assessment of consequences, fire setting is a common result.[19]

While strain theory focuses on the variables that explain the impetus for fire setting, routine activities theory highlights key environmental factors necessary to complete the act. Routine activities theory posits that the trifecta of a motivated offender, an available target, and a lack of supervision, results in criminal activity. Some youths engage in routine activities, such as spending afternoons hanging out at the mall or at friends' houses without parental supervision. In these situations, youths may encounter opportunities or targets for criminal activity. Coupled with an absence of supervision it is more likely that these youths will engage in criminal behavior. Indeed, some researchers argue that an increase in opportunities to engage in a criminal act without getting caught is a key component in explaining an increase in criminal behavior.[20] Consider, for example, a group of adolescents who are all equally interested in engaging in criminal activity. The youths in group A are regularly supervised by parents or coaches or other adults, while the youths in group B are often left on their own, unattended. Routine activities theory asserts that without any other motivators, the members of group B will engage in more deviant activity simply because they lack adult supervision. As it relates to fire setting behaviors, while a lack of supervision is problematic, access to fire ignition sources dramatically increases the chances that these youths will start a fire.[21]

Although sociological theory highlights important environmental factors related to fire setting behavior in some youths, it does not explain the phenomenon entirely. Despite their tendency to show aggression to others, fire setting adolescents generally lack assertiveness and problem solving skills. They are often social outcasts who have difficulty fitting into age-appropriate social groups and demonstrate an inability to form close friendships.[22] Given this, one might expect that these youth often report retaliation, revenge, and the desire to gain power as common motivations for starting fires.[23] Psychological diagnoses, such as conduct disorder, are common among juvenile fire setters and play an important role in understanding and treating these youngsters.

Psychological Factors
to Explain Firestarting

Early research suggests a similarity between the behaviors of fire setters and adolescents who were diagnosed with conduct disorder (CD).[24] According to the Diagnostic and Statistical Manual of Mental Disorders, Fourth Edition, Text Revision (DSM-IV-TR), conduct disorder is "a repetitive and persistent pattern of behavior in which the basic rights of others or major age-appropriate societal norms or rules are violated."[25] The specific violations include aggression, such as bullying and fighting, towards people or animals, the intentional destruction of property, deceitfulness, and consistent violation of rules.

While many adolescents get into fights or break the rules, children who are diagnosed with CD exhibit extreme forms of this otherwise normal adolescent rebellion. Children who set fires, however, display the most severe version of CD. When compared to their non-fire setting CD peers, they exhibit more aggression, theft, destruction of property, and lying.[26]

Other research has suggested that fire setting may co-occur with CD and is not simply an extreme form of the psychosis. When fire setters were compared with CD diagnosed non-fire setters, the fire setters exhibited pathologies above and beyond those normally associated with CD. Specifically, fire setters exhibited symptoms of *Psychasthenia* (a broad term used to describe obsessive behaviors), schizophrenia, and mania. The identification of schizophrenia in CD diagnosed fire setters is an important difference because it indicates an internalizing pathology marked by feelings of fear and worry that is not found in typical CD youths. This combined with the manic pathology, which usually involves excessive and irrational acting out behaviors, means there is a significant difference between CD and fire setting.[27]

Case Study
What's Up with Steve?

Given what you have read so far, what do we make of Steve's behavior? What sociological factors do you think contribute to his actions? What psychological issues is Steve likely wrestling with that manifest in his arsonist behavior? If you were a therapist and Steve was presented to you, what observations and conclusions might you draw from his situation?

A Typology of Fire Setters

As was mentioned, while much of the literature on fire setting is limited, one of the most important areas given empirical attention is the different types of fire setters. While it is easy to think of adult and juvenile fire setters as individuals who suffer from serious emotional disorders, there is a significant difference between adults who set fires and their juvenile counterparts. Additionally, even among juveniles, the motives behind setting fires are often quite varied. While there are a number of common factors found among juvenile fire setters, such as a history of family dysfunction, abuse, and neglect, it is worth noting that not all juveniles who set fires are equally motivated. Some experts have described four main types of juvenile fire setters, each with their own characteristics and motives for setting fires. They include curiosity fire setting, crisis fire setting, delinquent fire setting, and pathological fire setting.[28]

Curiosity Fire Setters

Curiosity fire setters have perhaps the most benign motives for committing these crimes. Some experts compare curiosity fire setting with fire play. This type of offender is generally curious about all things within their environment and is motivated by a desire to experiment. When youths throw toys, paper, or other things into a campfire simply to see what occurs, this might be considered a normal part of adolescent development. However, such individuals have very little understanding or appreciation of the danger their actions pose, and often find themselves shocked and overwhelmed by the destruction that occurs as a result. While fire setting can happen at any time and in any location, what makes curiosity fire setters so dangerous is that they often have little in the way of adult supervision and typically start fires in enclosed places, which accelerates the intensity of the fire, resulting in significant property damage and injury (see Table 4-2).

Table 4-2
Curiosity Fire Setters[29]

Personal Characteristics:
- Tend to be younger (ages 3–7).
- The vast majority (90%) are boys.
- High rate of impulsivity (ADHD).
- Are often non-verbal learners: learn by touching, experimenting, and manipulating, not by asking.
- Lack an appreciation of or understanding of a fire's dangerousness.
- Are often remorseful about their fire setting behavior.

Family Environment:
- Ready access to lighters and matches.
- One or more parents smoke.
- Poor supervision and parenting skills by adults in household.
- Limited parental understanding of fire safety (e.g. no smoke detectors, extinguishers or escape plans).

Types of Fires:
- Fires set in the home or nearby (e.g. backyard).
- Fires often set in hidden locations such as in a closet or under a bed.
- Typically use ordinary sources (e.g. matches or lighters) and accessible items to start fire (e.g. paper, toys).
- Often single episodes but can become a regular pattern.

Crisis Fire Setters

One of the areas in the empirical literature where experts agree relates to how youths often use fire as a coping mechanism to some type of crisis in their lives. In other words, in many cases, whether consciously or not, youths sometimes set fires in an effort to relieve the physical or emotional pain of some event that has taken place. In some ways, youths in this category are essentially trying to assert control that may be lacking in other areas of their lives, such as in their relationships with friends, teachers, and relatives.

Setting fires can be both psychologically healing as well as giving a particular youth some type of respect, admiration, or social standing in his or her social network. Thus, fires serve as empowering tools in an otherwise chaotic existence, and there is a social reward as an added bonus (see Table 4-3).

Table 4-3
Characteristics of Crisis Fire Setters[30]

Personal Characteristics:
- Predominantly boys (75–85%).
- Approximate ages 6–12 years old.
- History of physical, sexual, or emotional abuse.
- Socially isolated, loners, or frequently in conflict with peers.
- Little remorse for fire behavior or its impact on others.

Family Environment:
- Varied demographic and socioeconomic backgrounds.
- Some type of crisis or traumatic event as a precipitating event in fire setting.
- Can be episodic or a chronic crisis event.
- Resistant to intervention and change.

Types of Fires:
- Highly symbolic fires (e.g. they tell a story).
- Timing, location, sequence, and target of fires are important factors in understanding symbolic message.
- Fires not designed to hurt others.

Delinquent Fire Setters

Defiance and resistance to authority is a relatively normal part of adolescence. But what if the experience of growing up is an oppressive one for a youth? Is there some way to "get back" at those in authority positions? While delinquency covers a wide range of activities and the motives for engaging in various types of crime are far reaching, there are some youths who engage in setting fires as a result of anxiety, frustration, and revenge. Additionally, adolescence is a time when one's peer group holds considerable influence over the decision making of a particular youth. What is seen in this type of offender is more often a pattern of behavior, although single episodes can also occur. What is also seen is a more destructive, intentional motive for setting fires—this is not a cry for help or simply the result of curiosity. Rather, the delinquent fire setter is much more likely to be systematic in their fire setting activity.

While violence is often a topic of considerable interest to researchers who study delinquency, very little attention has been given to this type of offender.[31] Regardless of whether fire setting is a severe form of CD or a separate pathology, it is clear that the behavior regularly co-occurs with other psychological and familial issues. In addition to the diagnoses of CD and fire setting, children who display the most severe fire setting behaviors, those who set an average of 5.3 fires, are more likely to display a lack of remorse over their actions and a lack of empathy regarding the harm they caused (see Table 4-4).[32]

Table 4-4
Characteristics of Delinquent Fire Setters[33]

Personal Characteristics:
- Predominantly boys, but about 25–30% are girls.
- Approximate ages 10–17 years old.
- History of physical, sexual, or emotional abuse.
- Many meet criteria for conduct disorder or oppositional defiant disorder.
- Poorly developed social and interpersonal skills.
- Limited appreciation of dangerousness of fire, to self or others.
- Often motivated by revenge, anger, and intentional destruction of property.

Family Environment:
- Parents have high rates of domestic violence, substance abuse, and criminal activity.
- Parenting styles are highly rigid and punitive.
- Parents are resistant to social service providers.
- Inability to provide safe environment for child.

Types of Fires:
- Most often set outside home: schools, buildings, wooded areas, abandoned vehicles.
- Motive can be vandalism or revenge. Also, fires are used as an attempt to fit in with peers.
- Use of chemicals and explosive materials in setting fires.

Pathological Fire Setters

Finally there are pathological fire setters. These offenders are often the subject of media accounts because the nature of their fires is severe and significant. However, not only is the actual number of pyromaniacs and severely disturbed youths who set fires the smallest of all the categories mentioned, very few pathologically disturbed fire setters meet the criteria for pyromania. This is a disorder distinguished from other fire setting behaviors due to its diagnosis as an impulse disorder whereby individuals repeatedly set fires for the rush or excitement that comes from the fire itself.[34] This diagnosis is in contrast to other fire setters who use the fire as a means to an end.

Pathological fire setters who are not pyromaniacs are youths who suffer from serious emotional and psychological disorders, such as acute paranoia and delusional behavior. They are often actively psychotic, meaning they are currently in a mental state that does not allow them to distinguish reality from delusion.[35] They are typically youths who have lived in chronically disturbed environments for extended periods of time (e.g. profound deprivation, neglect, abuse, domestic violence, and substance abuse). In response to these conditions, many youths display a wide range of serious cognitive and neurological disorders that are likely to be permanent even with treatment (see Table 4-5).

Table 4-5
Characteristics of Pathological Fire Setters[36]

Personal Characteristics:
- Predominantly boys.
- Approximate ages 13–17 years old.
- History of physical, sexual, or emotional abuse.
- Evidence of paranoia, hallucinations, or delusions.
- Poorly developed problem solving, social, and interpersonal skills.
- Often have histories of early fascination with fire, which has been used as a coping mechanism.

Family Environment:
- Home life characterized by violence and abuse.
- Parents suffer from a variety of cognitive and emotional disorders.

- Family history of serious mental illness.

Types of Fires:
- High frequency of fire activity—often totaling hundreds of fires.
- Fire activities done alone or in secret.
- Fires are ritualistic in nature.
- Fires described in human terms (e.g. dancing, soothing).

In sum, the literature presents a broad profile of the juvenile fire setter. He is often a young male with a variety of psychological, social, and familial issues. He is regularly diagnosed with CD and generally exhibits more negative behaviors than non-fire setting CD youths. In the most severe circumstances he lacks empathy and requires inpatient treatment to address his tendency to set multiple fires. Given the complexity in diagnosing the root causes of fire setting behaviors, it follows that treating these youths is no easy task.

Intervention and Treatment Programs

As with the limited information available on the nature and motives of juvenile fire setting, there is limited empirical evidence regarding the effective treatment of youths who engage in this activity.[37] Most of the early studies on treatment focused almost exclusively on case studies and descriptions of programs designed for individual offenders. However, given the wide variability of fire setting activities and motives by offenders, such efforts were limited in their effectiveness. More recently, research on treatment focuses on three main areas: community-based treatment/education, cognitive-behavioral therapy, and residential treatment.

Research indicates that intervention and treatment programs for fire setting youths must be multi-dimensional. They must effectively educate those populations most at risk for fire setting behaviors, identify those youths who engage in fire play compared to fire setting, and treat them within the family. In the most extreme cases, intervention strategies may make use of inpatient treatment. In order to be successful these programs need to be cooperative efforts that include schools, juvenile justice programs, and other relevant community centers. Additionally, intervention programs must be age appropriate.[38]

For instance there are significant differences between child and teenage fire setters. Younger children are more likely to engage in spontaneous fire play and need interventions that discourage interest in those behaviors, encourage closer supervision of the child, and limit access to ignition sources.[39] Teenage fire setters, on the other hand, are likely to participate in repetitive fire setting that is characterized by both planned intention and secrecy. These youths may also be harder to identify and require more intensive interventions. Clearly, juvenile fire setters are a diverse group—what works with members of one group may not work with others.[40]

Community-Based Treatment and Education Programs

Community-based intervention programs became common in the late 1980s and early 1990s as the federal government recognized the extent of juvenile fire setting. The types of intervention strategies are designed to interrupt fire setting behavior. In most cases, these strategies promote quick responses when a juvenile engages in inappropriate fire behavior. Although systematic evaluations of intervention strategies are rare, the literature suggests that the more successful local efforts involve a combined response from the fire department, school, law enforcement, and mental health communities. Unfortunately little research exists that addresses the success of intervention efforts delimited by age of fire setter, type of fire setter, or event characteristics—all of which are important for determining best practices in fire setter interventions.[41]

The National Juvenile Firesetter/Arson Control and Prevention Program (NJF/ACP) was implemented during this time period by the Office of Juvenile Justice and Delinquency Prevention (OJJDP) and the U.S. Fire Administration. The NJF/ACP identified seven components as key to a community-focused prevention and treatment program:

1. A central organization that maintains contact with multiple service agencies.
2. A screening tool to assess children who are engaged in fire play.
3. An early intervention component.
4. A referral process whereby offenders can be linked to both individual and family services.
5. A public awareness campaign.
6. A means by which the effectiveness of the program can be measured.
7. A liaison to the juvenile justice agencies that often interact with juvenile fire setters.

These seven factors highlight key aspects of intervention treatment. They emphasize a multi-dimensional approach where individual and family counseling are used once children and teenagers are identified by a number of sources. This kind of broad network allows the community to identify and respond to potential fire threats in a variety of ways. It also ties treatment to research on the best practices of intervention. The effectiveness of juvenile fire setter programming has increased in communities where the NJF/ACP has been implemented.[42]

Programs that seek to educate young people regarding the dangers of fire play and fire setting should avoid scare tactics and instead emphasize a greater understanding of fire safety. For example, the Play Safe! Be Safe! program is a child-friendly curriculum implemented by the BIC pen corporation. The program is an interactive curriculum that uses games and storyboards to teach children about the consequences of fire play in an appropriate manner for three- to five-year-old children. Children who have completed the program demonstrate a greater knowledge of fire safety, including the fact that ignition sources (such as lighters and matches) should always be turned in to adults when found. Further, between 67% and 75% of children knew to call a firefighter in the event of a fire and to "stop, drop, and roll" under smoke. This outcome is significantly better than a comparison group who did not go through the program. Of those children, only 10% were able to display the same knowledge and skills.[43]

Media campaigns targeting fire prevention have a long-standing history. Smokey the Bear's iconic phrase "only you can prevent forest fires" has been uttered by children in America for decades. Smokey the Bear now has a website with games and stories that are similar in style to those found on the Play Safe! Be Safe! website. Recently, a crop of local agencies have begun to implement more specified programs. These programs concentrate the energies of primary, middle, and high schools on juveniles who are or have been identified as fire-involved in one way or another.

One example is Operation Extinguish in Montgomery County, MD. This model program was developed by the Department of Fire and Rescue Services in 1984 to provide intervention and educational services for juvenile fire setters and their families. The program combines psychological counseling and fire safety education and works to fully eliminate dangerous fire setting behaviors. In order to enter the program youths 7–18 years of age who are charged with arson are required to report to the Montgomery County Police Youth Division with their parents for screening. Applicants who are identified as appropriate for referral then undergo psychological evaluations (for both parent and child). Child and parent then participate in a series of education classes that focus on fire safety and mental health. This combination of community, family, and individual therapy has been successful in reducing fire setting behaviors and was named an outstanding juvenile justice program by the National Association of Counties.[44]

These community level interventions, particularly those that make use of existing social service agencies, make sense if one believes that fire setting is a product of routine activities and/or social strain theory. By emphasizing family, community, and the social context of youthful offenders, these programs are consistent with a sociological understanding of criminal behavior. In this light, the emphasis on teaching youths about the danger inherent in fire setting and providing them with social and emotional tools to avoid dangerous fire play is reasonable.

If, on the other hand, fire setting is considered to be more of a manifestation of a personality or behavioral disorder, then intensive psychological counseling and treatment programs are more appropriate. These therapies focus on behavior modification strategies such as consistent, controlled consequences for inappropriate behavior combined with positive reinforcement of desired behaviors, such as turning matchbooks or lighters in to parents/caretakers. The goal of these treatment methods is to address the child's conduct disorder by helping him or her to identify negative consequences of fire play while being encouraged by positive attention for positive behaviors.[45]

Cognitive-Behavioral Treatment

Cognitive-behavioral therapy (CBT) is generally considered by experts to be an effective therapeutic method.[46] The goal of CBT is to work with both the child and the family towards recognition that the setting of fires is a misguided attempt to communicate that is intensely meaningful for the child. By helping both the child and the family recognize that fire setting is purposeful, they can develop healthier strategies for self-expression and problem solving. CBT has been shown to be effective at helping children resist the urge to set fires by implementing alternative pathways to express frustration and attain desired goals.[47]

CBT is an intensive talk therapy program, where the patient is encouraged to identify their behaviors as consequences of their own thoughts, not the outside world. In this way the patient begins to feel a sense of internal control so that he or she can choose a course of action that is more socially acceptable.[48] Sessions are limited and intensive. The therapist attempts to gather information and interpret both verbal and non-verbal messages being communicated by the patient. As the sessions develop the therapist will challenge negative or inaccurate thinking in order to highlight the ways in which the offender has chosen his or her course of action and help them determine a healthier one in the future. These sessions help the child label stressors that led to the incident, label feelings that were generated by those stressors and the fire, and then analyze the consequences of the experience. In doing so the child is able to gain a sense of control over his or her emotions and actions.[49]

Residential Treatment

Residential treatment is used in those cases where the behavior is severe, chronic, and when other interventions have failed. Juvenile fire setters who have been sent to residential treatment facilities are perhaps the most serious offenders as well as those who suffer the most extreme effects of what led them to engaging in fire starting in the first place. That is, unlike curious fire setters, chronic offenders have more intense or prolonged experiences with family trauma, mental health issues, and a variety of other issues stemming from their fire setting activities.

The goal of residential treatment centers is essentially twofold: to terminate current and future fire setting behavior and to address the many problems, both internal and external, that a particular offender confronts. Experts generally consider the best way to accomplish these goals is by placing these types of offenders in a very structured and inflexible atmosphere that restricts their freedom. There are a wide range of therapeutic interventions employed in residential treatment, but the underlying factor in all of them is that the offender must learn to control their impulses and to develop a sense of self-discipline that allows them to resist engaging in fire setting behavior.

As was mentioned, in many ways, the motives for crisis fire setters and delinquent fire setters are different from youths who are simply curious about fire and set them "to see what happens." Those who knowingly and intentionally set fires for revenge, to destroy property, for profit, or as a result of a serious pathological disorder, are perhaps best treated in a therapeutic setting since it forces them to comply with rules and regulations (something chronic fire setters have difficulty accomplishing), as well as simultaneously addressing offenders' issues, including the trauma experienced from various forms of victimization.[50]

Summary

As was mentioned at the beginning of this chapter, relatively little is known or understood about juvenile fire setting. While more information has been obtained about the different types of offenders, as well as identifying some of the key issues surrounding the treatment of this behavior, many questions remain unanswered. In fact, the current level of understanding with regard to juvenile fire setting may be similar to society's understanding of child abuse more than 25 years ago. As experts and treatment professionals began to learn more about the long- and short-term effects of child abuse, research on the topic was only beginning to reveal the causes, risk factors, and effective treatment modalities to minimize the effects of abuse on children. Similarly, fire setting appears to be in a comparable stage of development, with no less importance in terms of its effects and correlations to other forms of delinquency.[51]

Notes

1. U.S. Department of Justice, Federal Bureau of Investigation, 2008. *Crime in the United States, Table 38* Washington, DC: U.S. Government Printing Office.

2. U.S. Department of Justice, Federal Bureau of Investigation. 2008. *Crime in the United States.* Washington, DC: U.S. Government Printing Office.

3. U.S. Department of Homeland Security, U.S. Fire Administration.2009. "Intentionally Set Fires." *Topical Fire Report Series* 9, 5: 1–9.

4. Raines, J. C. and Weigel Foy, C. 1994."Extinguishing the Fires Within: Treating Juvenile Firesetters," *Families in Society: The Journal of Contemporary Human Services* 75(10): 1433.

5. Hall, J. R. 2005. *Children Playing with Fire.* Quincy, MA: National Fire Protection Association.

6. U.S. Department of Justice, Federal Bureau of Investigation, 2008. *Crime in the United States.*

7. Ibid.

8. Ibid.

9. Putnam, C. T. and Kirkpatrick, J. T. 2005. *Juvenile Fire setting: A Research Overview.* Washington, DC: Office of Juvenile Justice Delinquency Prevention.

10. U.S. Fire Administration. 1998. "Technical Report Series, Special Report: Arson and Juveniles: Responding to the Violence," *USFA-TR-095,* January, http://www.usfa.dhs.gov/downloads/pdf/publications/tr-095.pdf.

11. Adapted from Putnam, C. T. and Kirkpatrick, J. T. 2005.

12. Tanenhaus, D. S. 2004. *Juvenile Justice in the Making: Studies in Crime and Public Policy.* New York: Oxford University Press.

13. Osborn, E. and Sakheim, G. A. 1999. "Severe vs. Nonsevere Firesetters Revisited," *Child Welfare* 78(4): 11–34.

14. Root, C., MacKay, S., Henderson, J., Del Bove, G., and Warling, E. 2008. "The Link Between maltreatment and juvenile firesetting: Correlates and underlying mechanisms" *Child Abuse & Neglect* 32(2): 161–176.

15. Tanenhaus, 2004.

16. Ibid.

17. Root, MacKay, Henderson, Del Bove, and Warling. 2008.

18. Ibid.

19. Raines, J. and Weigel Foy, 1994.

20. Cohen , L. E. and Felson, M. 2009. "Routine Activity Theory" in Cullen, F. T. and Agnew, R. 2009 (eds.), *Criminological Theory: Past to Present. Essential Readings,* 2009. Los Angeles, CA: Roxbury Publishing.

21. Raines, J. and Weigel Foy, 1994.

22. Office of Juvenile Justice and Delinquency Prevention. 1997. *Juvenile Firesetting and Arson. Fact Sheet 51.*; U.S. Fire Administration /Federal Emergency Management Agency. 1993. *The National Juvenile Fire setter /Arson Control and Prevention Program Fire Service Guide to a Juvenile Fire setter Early Intervention Program*; U.S. Fire Administration /Federal Emergency Management Agency. 1997. *Arson and Juveniles: Responding to the Violence. A Review of Teen Fire setting and Interventions, Special Report.*

23. Osborn and Sakheim, 1999.
24. Kolko, D. J., Kazdin, A. E., and Meyer, E. C. 1985. "Aggression and Psychopathology in Childhood Firesetters: Parent and Child Reports," *Journal of Consulting and Clinical Psychology*, 53(3): 377–385.
25. American Psychiatric Association, *Diagnostic and Statistical Manual of Mental Disorders DSM-IV-TR Fourth Edition (Text Revision)* (Washington, DC: American Psychiatric Publishing, Inc.; 4th edition 2000).
26. Kolko, Kazdin, and Meyer, 1985.
27. Moore, J. M., Thompson-Pope, S. K., and Whited, R. M. 1996. "MMPI-A Profiles of Adolescent Boys with a History of Firesetting." *Journal of Personality Assessment*, 67(1): 116–126.
28. See Stadolink, R. F. 2000. *Drawn to the Flame: Assessment and Treatment of Juvenile Firesetting Behavior.* Sarasota, FL: Professional Resources Press. See also Kolko, D. (ed.) 2002. *Handbook on Fire setting in Children and Youth.* Boston, MA: Academic Press.
29. Adapted from Stadolnik, R. F. 2000, pp. 22–28.
30. Ibid.
31. Ibid.
32. Moore, Thompson-Pope, and Whited, 1996.
33. Adapted from Stadolnik, 2000, pp. 22–28.
34. American Psychiatric Association, 2000.
35. Ibid.
36. Adapted from Stadolnik, 2000, pp. 22–28.
37. Kolko, D. J. 2002. "Research Studies on the Problem," in Kolko, D. J. (ed.). *Handbook on Firesetting in Children and Youth.* San Diego, CA: Academic Press.
38. Sharp, D. L., Blaakman, S., Cole, E. and Cole, R. 2005, "Evidence-Based Multidisciplinary Strategies for Working With Children Who Set Fires," *Journal of the American Psychiatric Nurses Association*, 11(6): 329–337.
39. Ibid.
40. Rock, P. and MacIntosh, M. 1972. "Labeling Theory Reconsidered," in Rock, P. and MacIntosh, M. (eds.). *Deviance and Social Control.* London: Tavistock.
41. Ibid.

42. Garry, E. M. 1997. "Juvenile Firesetting." *Office of Juvenile Justice and Delinquency Prevention Fact Sheet #51*, http://owl.english.purdue.edu/owl/resource/717/04/.

43. Sharp, Blaakman, Cole, and Cole, 2005.

44. Montgomery County, MD, "Safety in Our Neighborhood," *Montgomery County Operation Extinguish, 2008*, http://www.montgomerycountymd.gov/content/frs-safe/resources/parents/operationextinguish.asp.

45. Raines and Weigel Foy, 1994.

46. See for instance Stadolnik, R. F.; Kolko 2002.

47. Kolko, 2002.

48. Ibid.

49. O'Donohue, W. T. and Fisher, J. E. 2003. *Cognitive Behavior Therapy: Applying Empirically Supported Techniques in Your Practice* Hoboken, NJ: Wiley.

50. Kolko, D. J. 2002. "Research Studies on the Problem," in Kolko, D. J. (ed.). *Handbook on Firesetting in Children and Youth.* San Diego, CA: Academic Press.

51. Putnam and Kirkpatrick, 2005.

Chapter 5

Juvenile Domestic Violence

Case Studies in Delinquency

Thomas and Jane are a high school couple who have been together since their sophomore year. Their friends Melissa and Tavaris, who have just started dating, are joining them at a party to celebrate Homecoming. Thomas is the designated driver for the evening, but the other three have been drinking and are generally enjoying themselves. There are no adults at the celebration. Thomas and Jane get into an argument when Jane's ex-boyfriend arrives unannounced. In the midst of the argument Thomas loses his temper and begins calling Jane names in front of the entire party. Jane begins to yell as well, and the conflict escalates, with Thomas hitting Jane, breaking her nose. Someone at the party calls the police and Melissa and Tavaris decide to leave the party before officers arrive (the police eventually arrested and charged Thomas with aggravated assault).

They head to Tavaris's home. His father has recently been diagnosed with stage III cancer, and the effects of the illness have been hard on the family, with tensions running high about finances, the impending loss of the head of the family, and an inability to resolve conflict effectively.

After arriving at Tavaris's home, Tavaris's brother Robert and Tavaris get into an argument about keeping the house neat and tidy. Not satisfied with Tavaris's responses, Robert begins to push Tavaris around. The situation degenerates into a violent confrontation, where Robert hits Tavaris with several punches to the face, all the while leveling insults at him. Tavaris receives a black eye and a sprained wrist. Melissa wants to call the police and file a claim against Robert, but Tavaris shrugs off the incident, claiming that this is how his family solves problems.

Questions to Consider:

1. Who do you think is at a greater risk for being the victim of violence in this situation, Jane or Thomas?
2. Because they have just started dating, are Melissa and Tavaris more or less likely to experience violence in their relationship?
3. Thomas is known for his bad temper and has hit Jane in the past. Is he just a guy with a short fuse or is his violence rooted in social causes?
4. Was Tavaris the victim of domestic violence? Should Robert be arrested?

In the United States, people tend to victimize those closest to them—this is sometimes referred to as *intimate partner violence*. Intimate partner violence refers to the physical, sexual, and/or emotional harm caused by one's romantic partner. Psychological abuse, another form of victimization, includes humiliating a partner in front of friends, threatening physical violence, and limiting contact with peers. Physical violence can include scratching, slapping, bending fingers, choking, burning, hitting with fists, or the use of other weapons. Sexual violence can range from forced touching to coerced intercourse.[1]

According to the Uniform Crime Reports, in 2009 about 40% of all homicides were perpetrated by a romantic partner or family member.[2] While many discussions of domestic violence focus on adult perpetrators in the context of marriage or family (i.e., spousal abuse or child abuse), the literature suggests the issue is much more complex and pervasive. On the other hand, there is some truth to the perception that romantically involved adults are especially violent: most perpetrators of domestic violence are between the ages of 18 and 35,[3] and women are 13 times more likely to be injured by a domestic partner than by a stranger.[4]

What is missing from these statistics, however, is the reality of violence committed against family members and romantic partners by persons under the age of 18, what we will refer to as *juvenile domestic violence*. This includes young victims as well as offenders. For example, children are more likely to be the victims of physical and/or sexual violence at the hands of siblings than their parents or guardians.[5] Furthermore, as many as 40% of dating teenagers report using violence against their partner.[6] In this chapter we discuss domestic violence within families and between romantic partners, focusing initially on the prevalence of domestic violence in general as well as sibling abuse, child to parent violence, and dating violence. As the family is generally considered to be a training ground for violent behaviors, we explore the link between family violence and intimate partner violence. This chapter concludes with a discussion of institutional responses to intimate partner violence among adolescent populations.

The Nature of Family Violence

"Family violence" is an umbrella term that includes child physical and sexual abuse, child neglect and maltreatment, intimate partner violence, and elder abuse. Some experts contend that intimate partner violence, which includes domestic violence, is the most common violent crime in the United States.[7] For example, data indicates that 1 in every 4 women will experience domestic violence in her lifetime. Additionally, it is estimated that about 4.8 million incidents of physical assault by an intimate partner occur each year and 75% of those victims are females. Of all the women murdered in the United States, about one-third were killed by an intimate partner.[8] The public is generally misinformed about the nature of domestic violence—in fact, several myths about family violence pervade the public's thinking about the nature of this activity (See Figure 5-1).

What is interesting is that children who witness abuse often have the same types of problems as those who experience it. For example, children who witness abuse often suffer from low self esteem, depression, stress disorders, poor impulse control, and feelings of powerlessness. They are also at high risk for alcohol and drug use, sexual acting out, running away, isolation, fear, and suicide.[9] Sadly, children exposed to such violence at an early age are likely to be-

---

Figure 5-1
Family Violence Myths

Myth: *Family Violence Rarely Occurs.*
Although statistics on family violence are not precise, it is clear that millions of children, women and even men are abused physically by family members and other intimates.
Myth: *Family Violence Only Happens in Low-income Families.*
Reports from police records, victim services, and academic studies show domestic violence exists equally in every socioeconomic group, regardless of race or culture.
Myth: *Alcohol and Drugs Cause Family Violence.*
Domestic violence and substance abuse are related, but really are two different problems. The evidence on domestic violence shows that most offenders, who typically are male, find a time and place to victimize wives or girlfriends when others will not witness it. This happens whether he is drunk/high or not. While being drunk may be used as an excuse for the abusive behavior, it is not a causal factor in explaining how or why it occurs.
Myth: *Battered Spouses Can Leave If They Really Want To.*
Often, batterers create a sense of social and economic dependency in their victims. Isolated from friends, family, and economic resources, when the decision to flee is made, the victim often realizes he or she has very little in the way of money, job skills, or friends. This says nothing of the fear of physical retaliation the victim may feel if he or she leaves the abusive partner.
Source: "Preventing Violence Against Women, Not Just a Women's Issue," National Crime Prevention Council.

---

come either perpetrators of abuse or victims of violence in adulthood.[10] In fact, boys who have witnessed abuse of their mothers are 10 times more likely to batter their female partners as adults.[11]

Consider some other facts about the impact of family violence:

- Children of battered women are fifteen times more likely to be battered themselves than children whose mothers are not abused.

- Because the abuser often uses the children's behavior as an excuse for battering the woman, children often blame themselves for their mother's abuse.

- Divorced and separated women, who compose only 10% of all women, account for 75% of all battered women and report being battered 14 times as often as women still living with their partners.[12]

In trying to make sense of family violence, particularly as it relates to children, many experts agree that it involves a *cycle of violence*, where parents and caretakers discipline their children using violence because that is the way they were raised. The upshot, of course, is that victims of such abuse become violent offenders themselves as they get older.[13] A young person who is a victim of neglect or abuse is more likely to become a delinquent than one who is not mistreated. For instance, one study compared the arrest records of 908 abused or neglected children, age 11 or younger at the time of abuse or neglect, with arrest records for 667 children who were not abused or maltreated. The study found that "being abused or neglected as a child increased the likelihood of arrest as a juvenile by 59% as an adult by 28% and for a violent crime by 30%."[14] Additionally, children who do not become offenders or victims may face great obstacles in emotional, mental, and physical development. These obstacles include attention deficits, educational difficulties, substance abuse, mental health problems, symptoms of post-traumatic stress disorder, and lack of appropriate social skills.[15]

Corporal Punishment as Family Violence

Another dimension of family violence relates to the use of corporal punishment as a disciplinary tool. While in an earlier time many people believed that "sparing the rod spoils the child," today, even though most people in the United States approve of spanking, the issue remains a controversial one. What is the difference between punishment and discipline? Although the two are related and often used together, as a general rule, *discipline* is a tool that parents and other adults use to effectively socialize and teach children about boundaries and limitations. *Punishment*, on the other hand, places less emphasis on teaching and more on accountability for misbehavior. So discipline is proactive, and it includes all the means that parents use to guide their children's behavior: setting limits, stating consequences, providing positive role models, and reinforcement for good behavior. Punishment, on the other hand, happens after the fact and acknowledges only misbehavior.

Spanking can include a range of corporal punishments, from simply hitting the child on the buttocks to slapping the child's hand or face. Murray Straus, a well-known researcher in the field of family violence, defines *corporal punishment* as the use of physical force with the intention of causing bodily pain, but not injury, for the purpose of correction or control.[16] Corporal punishment that causes injury is by definition child abuse.

Many psychologists and pediatricians say that parents should never strike a child. Researchers generally agree that frequent and impulsive spanking, hitting children with objects, or even yelling at them, are detrimental to their development and can lead to delinquency and even adult crime. According to Alan Kazdin, professor of psychology at Yale University, "Children who are hit become more aggressive."[17] According to the American Academy of Pediatrics, spanking can escalate into physical abuse and contribute to later emotional and behavioral problems. Many recent studies show that spanking is linked to higher rates of domestic violence and assault.[18]

How Often Do We Actually Spank Our Children?

Despite the debate about the acceptability and effectiveness of corporal punishment, the reality is that its use has remained controversial, but appears to be subsiding. While corporal punishment of toddlers has not decreased, severity levels have subsided and the age at which it ends has declined as well. This may be due to the influence of the media and the lack of the social acceptability of spanking, but regardless, spanking appears to be used less often as a disciplinary tool. In a 2002 *ABC News* poll, 65% of Americans polled said they approve of spanking children, which had remained the same since 1990. About half of parents say they sometimes spank their own kids, similar to findings in a 1990 Gallup poll. There were some variations in spanking, such as Southerners being more likely to spank than other regions of the country, as well as there being a difference based on education levels: only 38% of parents with college degrees spanked their kids, while 55% of less-educated parents used spanking as a disciplinary tool.

Source: Diaz, J., Peddle, N., Reid, R., & Wang, C. (2002). *Current trends in child abuse prevention and fatalities: The 2000 fifty state survey.* Chicago, IL: Prevent Child Abuse America.

Cite 40

Perhaps the most compelling argument against spanking is that it simply does not work. If the objective behind spanking is to change behavior of children, other disciplinary tactics are more effective and less traumatic.[19] On the other hand, some psychologists argue that low levels of corporal punishment are acceptable, do no long-term damage, and can be an effective disciplinary tool. While advocates of spanking argue it is always better to provide correction through explanation, light spanking may reinforce other forms of correction, such as a time out.[20] Most experts warn parents against not only spanking but also against verbal assault, yelling at or disparaging children. Frequent verbal reprimands become ineffective and reinforce undesired behavior. Verbal hostility may actually lead to more detrimental consequences for the child than does even physical abuse. One study of more than 3,000 parents and their children younger than 18 years of age linked both verbal and physical aggression by parents to aggressive behavior, delinquency, and interpersonal problems in their children. The psychological abuse, in fact, was the more harmful of the two. Those connections applied to both boys and girls, regardless of age.[21]

The Social Acceptability of Intrafamily Violence

Despite the commonly held perception that corporal punishment or spanking is an acceptable disciplinary tool, and despite the attention given to domestic violence in this country, the American family remains a violent institution. In the late 1960s President Johnson formed the National Commission on the Causes and Prevention of Violence. The purpose of this commission was to understand the circumstances under which the average American would approve of using violent actions. The study found that 25% of men and nearly 17% of women could identify a situation in which they would approve of a husband slapping his wife. Additionally, 93% had experienced physical punishment as a child.[22] Although these numbers have fluctuated somewhat over the past 40 years, the American family remains a site of conflict and physical harm.

Some experts suggest that we ought not be surprised by the violent nature of the American family.[23] Parents, siblings, and spouses sometimes feel as though they possess a right to control or influence their family members and may feel insulted or snubbed when their influence is inhibited in some way. These frustrations are amplified by the limited resources available to some family members, where parents, siblings and spouses must compete for attention, goods and services (such as the family car), or even financial support. While all of these factors can be a source of conflict, not all of them lead to violence.

Additionally, the extent of violence within families is based in part on how one defines it. For example, consider a family where two boys wrestle with one another—is this family violence? What if it was in response to a dispute or argument? What about a husband who slaps his wife? How about a homosexual man who slaps his partner? Are all of these actions equally violent? The point is that the definition of what constitutes violence varies considerably, making the public's perceptions difficult to determine.

The complexity of family violence can be generally understood as it relates to three dimensions:

Dimensions of Violence[24]	
Instrumental	Violence that is used to achieve a purpose, such as to get a partner or child to start/stop a certain behavior or to assert or regain control.
Expressive	Violence that is used to communicate one's feelings, as in pushing in a burst of anger or slapping to express hurt.
Legitimate	Violence that is legally permissible, such as spanking a child in a manner that does not leave a bruise or welt.
Illegitimate	Violence that is outside the realm of legal behavior, such as rape or murder.

Victim-precipitated	Violent behavior in response to the other's actions.
Not-victim-precipitated	Violent behavior that is not spurred on by the victim.

These categories are useful in that they distinguish between a sibling argument that escalates to a violent confrontation or to a criminal act. These dimensions are also helpful as the discussion shifts to certain types of family violence, such as sibling abuse, child to parent violence, or dating violence.

Sibling Abuse

Sibling abuse, the intentional emotional, physical, or sexual abuse of a child by his or her brother or sister, is likely the most common form of intra-family conflict.[25] We say this because such activity is difficult to measure. Victims often do not identify the behavior as abusive or violent and a certain amount of teasing, arguing and fighting by siblings is considered acceptable by many people even when it involves a physical altercation.[26]

For example, according to Murray Strauss' Conflict Tactics Scale, as many as 80% of respondents have suffered sibling abuse.[27] In one study 47.8% of respondents reported having suffered physical aggression from a sibling while 40.9% admitted to having perpetrated violence against a sibling. However, of those who were victimized, less than 10% considered the violence to be abusive at the time. Even in retrospect, when victims became adults and looked back on those experiences, less than one in five (19.6%) labeled the experience as abusive.[28]

This lack of recognition does not mean a form of abuse and victimization did not occur. Sibling violence is not merely an innocent rite of passage and it regularly involves violence that goes beyond a wrestling match: about 3 out of 100 children used a weapon when assaulting their siblings.[29] Distinguishing between sibling rivalry/tension and sibling abuse is further complicated by the fact that many victims of sibling violence (31.5%) also reported being a perpetrator of violence.[30]

Despite the murky nature of victim and parent reporting practices, some trends regarding abusive siblings are evident. At first glance, boys are more likely than girls to engage in violent behavior, and older children are less likely to be aggressive toward their siblings. Parents who are considering a separation or divorce, as well as parents with a low family income, are more likely to have children who victimize their siblings.

Perhaps even more important in understanding and predicting sibling abuse are the ways in which parents interact with their children: the frequency of a father losing his temper with his children, whether a mother uses corporal punishment on her children, or if either parent is violent toward their child, all increase the likelihood of that child inflicting abuse upon a sibling.[31]

Child to Parent Violence

The rate of child to parent violence is relatively low, which may account for the lack of attention this issue has received in the academic literature. Approximately 7–11% of sophomore, junior, or senior males report that they have hit one or both of their parents.[32] What research exists on this topic indicates that mothers are the most likely victims of child aggression and single mothers are more at risk than married mothers.[33] White males are more likely to engage in child to parent violence than black males or females of any race.[34] The majority of child offenders do not have a clinical diagnosis, although behavior disorders and acting out in school are positively associated with child to parent violence.[35]

The nature of child to parent violence varies from threats to physical altercations. The data indicate that most child-initiated violence begins between the ages of 12 and 16. The level of violence varies, apparently according to the size of the child. Larger, stronger, or taller boys tend to use intimidation, while smaller or weaker boys will engage in more severe forms of violence, even to the point of using weapons.[36]

The research is nearly unanimous in its finding that children who engage in violence towards their parents have first been the victims of violence. Given this history of child abuse among this population of offenders, the violence is thought to be instrumental, i.e., as a means for stopping the abuse. Specifically, children who are abused by their parents are more likely to be violent towards their parents, and children who are violent towards their parents reduce the likelihood of suffering further abuse.[37] In this way, child to parent violence may be viewed as a rational and effective means for reducing the negative experience of child abuse.

Juvenile Dating Violence

While intra-family violence is problematic at a number of levels, intimate partner violence among young people is not limited to family members. As was mentioned, violence in romantic relationships is dishearteningly common and teenagers involved in intimate relationships are not immune to this trend. Not only do over one-quarter of dating teens perpetrate physical violence on their partners, a majority report suffering emotional abuse and as many as 15% report being forced into sexual relations.[38] In addition to the obvious negative emotional and physical consequences of such circumstances, being in a violent dating relationship is positively associated with inconsistent condom use and unplanned pregnancies.[39] So what causes teenagers to engage in this kind of unhealthy behavior?

As we begin, consider the many factors that contribute to a teen's decision to inflict violence upon their partner: the level of parental involvement in the youth's life, the social acceptability of the use of violence in that family, and whether or not the youth has friends who think violence is acceptable. All of these factors contribute to the decision to use violence as a problem-solving tool in an intimate relationship.

Theoretically social learning theory offers important insight into the nature of dating violence. Social learning theory essentially states that we all learn from parents or peers or other significant influences to define certain behaviors as normative and acceptable and others as inappropriate. If an individual holds a definition of violence as an acceptable, even useful, means of resolving conflict then she or he is more likely to engage in violent behaviors.[40]

The data suggests that both young men and women hold positive perceptions of dating violence when their parents communicate support for aggressive solutions to conflict. Additionally, spending time with deviant peers positively influences both sexes' perceptions of dating violence.[41] The relationship between others' positive definitions of aggressive conflict resolution and one's own definitions appears to be stronger for girls than for boys. The data suggests that only young women report a significant relationship between parents' support for non-violent solutions and their own negative perception of intimate partner violence.[42] Put another way, kids are strongly influenced by their parents' beliefs and attitudes about using violence as a means to resolve conflicts. Parents who support the use of aggressive behavior or violence are more likely to have children, boys or girls, who hold a favorable attitude towards violence in dating relationships.

Finally, one of the most hotly debated aspects of intimate partner violence among teenagers is girls who identify themselves as *perpetrators* of violence.[43] In one study 29% of women reported being the perpetrator of violence in the relationship. The explanation for this trend may be similar to that used for males who engage in violence. Youths, particularly women, who learn positive attitudes regarding the use of violence to resolve conflict are more likely to engage in violence. In fact, this aggression is generally evident in multiple relationships. Youths who are aggressive towards a parent or romantic partner are much more likely to be aggressive towards same age and same sex peers as well.[44] The Centers for Disease Control have found that in addition to physical altercations with peers, being sexually active, having attempted suicide, and engaging in heavy drinking, are all risk factors associated with teen intimate partner violence.[45]

Explaining Family Violence

Although it remains a very complex topic, with a host of issues to consider, the explanation of family violence can be seen through four sociological lenses. These theories apply to family violence in general or to specific forms of family violence, such as sibling abuse or even dating violence.

Table 5-1
Sociological Theories of Family Abuse[46]

Feminist Theory	Patriarchal structures place men in positions of power, thereby condoning violence against women or the less powerful.
Conflict Theory	Violence is used as a means to resolve the tension that results from competing interests within a family.
Strain Theory	Children raised in families where they are exposed to negative stimuli will respond with deviant, or violent, behaviors.
Social Learning Theory	Parents who model violence teach children that it is an acceptable or appropriate tool for resolving conflict.

Feminist theories of crime call attention to the importance of understanding gender when considering criminal or deviant acts. Gender not only influences society's interpretation of deviant acts (such as the difference in the social acceptability of seeing two boys fighting compared to two girls), but it can also influence a perpetrator's decision to engage in criminal behavior. Specifically, feminists argue that there exists in society a patriarchal social structure where, to varying degrees, men hold (and expect to hold) positions of power while women play supportive or submissive roles. In the context of these unequal power relationships, men may perceive violent or controlling behavior as appropriate; much as a parent must discipline a child, or a boss must monitor an employee, so must the husband/boyfriend/ brother monitor, supervise, and correct the women in his life.[47]

Within this patriarchal social structure violence against women becomes normative or acceptable. Feminists note data that suggests gender, specifically being male, has an indirect effect on the likelihood of violence. Additionally, having a brother who favors the division of chores along traditional gender lines (boys mow the lawn, girls do the dishes) significantly increases the likelihood of sibling violence. The data also indicates that males are more likely than females to report using violence as a means of resolving family conflict amongst siblings.[48] Furthermore, sibling pairs that consist of a male older sibling and female younger sibling report the greatest amount of conflict and violence.[49] Where feminist theory falls short of the mark relates to a common finding in the literature on sibling abuse: brothers are more likely to report sibling violence than any other sibling combination.

Conflict theories of crime suggest that the source of sibling and family violence may be the result of competing interests. When parents favor one sibling over another, for example, violence increases. Specifically, this favoritism complicates the lives of siblings as they attempt to share resources such as toys, space, and parental affection. Thus, the competition between siblings, which is most likely to become violent between boys, is the consequence of the perceived limits to parental affection.[50]

General strain theory explains how the presence of generalized negative stimuli can exacerbate already volatile family relationships. Agnew's general strain theory argues that an individual will engage in deviant behaviors as a means of escaping, stopping or alleviating the stress induced by negative stimuli such as abuse or stressful life events.[51] General strain theory helps us to understand that family stressors, such as financial strain or illness, are significantly related to increased violence.[52] In this sense the violence is essentially a reaction to the generalized stress of financial hardship or illness.

All of these theories struggle to identify the mechanism by which an individual chooses to engage in violence. That is, we live in a patriarchal society in this country and many children perceive themselves to be in competition, at one level or another, with their siblings, and most families experience external stressors. Why do some people take the next step and become violent while others employ strategies of peaceful coexistence? Indeed, in studies of sibling conflict, non-violent means (such as yelling or ignoring) are the most common strategies reported by both males and females.[53]

Social learning theory offers perhaps the most compelling explanation of family violence. The research consistently demonstrates that children who grow up in homes with high levels of parental conflict report higher levels of sibling violence.[54] Indeed, in families where there is conflict between parents there is also an increased likelihood of parents yelling at or abusing children. Those negative parent-child interactions result in increased instances of violent conflict between siblings. In this sense children mimic the positive definitions their parents have of using violence as a means of conflict resolution.

Social learning theory also helps us to understand instances of child to parent violence as well. As was mentioned, the rate of child to parent violence is relatively low, with approximately 7–11% of high school sophomores, juniors, or seniors reporting that they have hit one or both of their parents.[55] Youths who are emotionally attached to their parents and whose parents are more likely to agree with one another are less likely to engage in child to parent violence. Those youths who have learned positive definitions of violence by watching their parents, however, are more likely to mimic that violence as adolescents. Children who reported that their parents used either a primarily punitive or primarily violent style of interaction were more likely to have hit their parents than their peers who were raised using more non-punitive or peaceful interaction styles.[56]

Addressing Domestic Violence

The most obvious answer to addressing family violence involves the criminal justice system. However, for many years the police were limited in what they could do to address domestic violence.

It was not until criminologist Larry Sherman's landmark study was publicized that the way of addressing family violence changed. Sherman's work demonstrated a positive impact of police intervention on rates of domestic violence. Historically, police officers only arrested perpetrators of domestic violence when the victim was willing to press charges. This tactic proved to be ineffective as victims were often unwilling, perhaps because of fear of retaliation or abandonment, to press charges. Sherman demonstrated that future incidences of violence were reduced when the perpetrator was removed from the scene and the officer became the complainant and was able to make an arrest regardless of victim cooperation.[57]

Sherman's later work, however, qualified the mandatory arrest action.[58] He and his colleagues found that persons who were not married and did not have gainful employment were more likely to engage in repeat intimate partner violence than their counterparts who were not arrested. In other words, the deterrence of arrest only worked for persons who were either married or had jobs. Sherman concluded that this was due to the integration of the individual into the community—that is, either through marriage or through gainful employment, a person is more likely to feel the pain of arrest than persons who are not connected to the community. It is unclear what these new findings suggest about pro-arrest policies for juveniles.

What impact did this change in thinking and understanding the nature of violence have on juvenile crime? Fights with parents or siblings that had previously been ignored by law enforcement, or in which the youth had been charged with the status offense of incorrigibility or ungovernability, now resulted in an arrest for simple or aggravated assault. According to some estimates, by the late 1990s, it was not uncommon for as many as one-third of all juveniles referred to court for a violent crime to be charged with domestic violence.[59]

Case Studies in Delinquency
Conclusions about Melissa and Tavaris

Given what you have learned about sibling violence, is what happened between Robert and Tavaris simply a case of boys being boys? Given the acceptability of violence as a problem-solving tool in Tavaris's family, do you think Melissa is in danger? What about the conflict between Thomas and Jane—was it an isolated incident or part of a pattern? Is Jane in any danger of being harmed in the future?

Summary

The study of intimate partner violence is a complex issue that includes topics such as sibling violence, dating violence and children who inflict violence upon their parents. Part of the solution to this type of criminal activity is found in understanding its causes. While there may be a variety of macro-level theories to explain why it occurs, in the end, intimate partner violence, whether it be intra-family or romantic, involves a learned set of behaviors. When youths watch their parents argue and fight, when they are physically punished themselves by their parents, or when they are encouraged to use violence themselves as a problem-solving tool, they learn positive definitions of violence.[60] Increasingly, the criminal justice system is being called upon to address this issue and the question remains whether this is the appropriate mechanism to resolve this issue, particularly among victims and offenders under the age of 18.

Notes

1. James, W. H., West, C., Ezrre Deters K., and Eduardo, A. 2000. "Youth Dating Violence." *Adolescence*, 35(139): 455–465.

2. http://www2.fbi.gov/ucr/cius2009/offenses/expanded_information/data/shrtable_10.html.

3. http://www.ncjrs.gov/pdffiles1/nij/225722.pdf.

4. Sappinton, A. A., Pharr, R., Tunstall, A., and Rickert, E. 1977. "Relationships Among Child Abuse, Date Abuse, and Psychological Problems." *Journal of Clinical Psychology*, 53(4): 319–329.

5. Finkelhor D., Ormrod R., Turner H., Hamby S. L. 2005. "The Victimization of Children and Youth: A Comprehensive, National Survey." *Child Maltreatment*, 10(1): 5–25.

6. Miller, S., Gorman-Smith, D., Sullivan, T., Orpinas, P., Simon, T. R. 2009. "Parent and Peer Predictors of Physical Dating Violence Perpetration in Early Adolescence: Tests of Moderation and Gender Differences." *Journal of Clinical Child and Adolescent Psychology*, 38(4): 538–550.

7. Redden, G. 2008. *Violence in the Family*. National Association of Children of Alcoholics. http://www.nacoa.org/famviol.htm.

8. Bureau of Justice Statistics, 2007. *Homicide Trends in the U.S.* Washington, DC: U.S. Department of Justice. http://www.ojp.gov/bjs/homicide/intimates.htm.

9. Redden, G. 2008.

10. Bureau of Justice Statistics. 2000. *Intimate Partner Violence*, Washington, DC: U.S. Department of Justice. http://www.ojp.usdoj.gov/bjs/pub/pdg/jpv.pdf retrieved February 3, 2009.

11. Redden, G. 2008.

12. Ibid.

13. Department of Justice, Office of Juvenile Justice Delinquency Prevention. 2001. *The Nurturing Parenting Programs*. Washington, D.C. http://www.ncjrs.gov/pdffiles1/ojjdp/172848.pdf retrieved February 3, 2009.

14. National Institute of Justice. 2001. An Update on the Cycle of Violence. Washington, DC. Available at http://www.ncjrs.gov/pdffiles1/ojjdp/184894.pdf.

15. U.S. Department of Justice, Office of Juvenile Justice and Delinquency Prevention. 2000. *Safe From the Start: Taking Action on Children Exposed to Violence*, Washington, DC. Available at http://www.ncjrs.gov/pdffiles1/ojjdp/182789.pdf.

16. Straus, M. A. 1993. *Ten Myths About Spanking Children*. New Hampshire: Family Research Laboratory, University of New Hampshire.

17. Harder, B. 2007. "When parents lift their hands." http://articles.latimes.com/2007/feb/19/health/he-spanking19 retrieved July 17, 2008.

18. Ibid.

19. Ibid.

20. Ibid.

21. Harder 2007.

22. Gelles, R. and Stauss, M. A. 1979. "Determinants of violence in the family: Toward a theoretical integration" in F. I. Nye and I.L. Reiss (Eds.) *Contemporary Theories About the Family* New York: Free Press.

23. Ibid.

24. Jackman, M. R. 2002. "Violence in Social Life." *Annual Review of Sociology*, 28: 387–415.

25. Straus, M. A., Gelles, R. J., and Steinmetz, S. K. 1980. *Behind Closed Doors: Violence in the American Family.* Garden City, New York: Doubleday.

26. Gelles, R. J. and Cornell, C. P. 1985. *Intimate Violence in Families.* Beverly Hills: Sage.

27. Straus, M. A. and Gelles, R. J. 1990. "How violent are American families? Estimates from the National Family Violence Resurvey and other studies." In M. Straus & R. Gelles (Eds.), *Physical violence in American families: Risk Factors and Adaptations to Violence in Families* (pp. 95–112). New Brunswick, NJ: Transaction.

28. Ibid.

29. Graham-Bermann S., Cutler, S. E., Litzenberger, B. W., and Schwartz, W. E. 1994. *Perceived Conflict and Violence in Childhood Sibling Relationships and later Emotional Adjustment.*" Journal of Family Psychology, 8(1): 85–97.

30. Hardy, M. S. 2001. "Physical Aggression and Sexual Behavior Among Siblings: A Retrospective Study." *Journal of Family Violence,* 16(3): 255–268.

31. Eriksen, S. and Jensen, V. 2006. "All in the Family? Family Environment Factors in Sibling Violence." *Journal of Family Violence,* 21: 497–507.

32. Peek, Charles W., Fischer, J. L., and Kidwell, J. S. (1985). "Teenage Violence Towards Parents: A Neglected Dimension of Family Violence." *Journal of Family Violence.*

33. Agnew, R. & Huguley, S. (1989). Adolescent violence towards parents. *Journal of Marriage and the Family,* 51(3): 699–711.

34. Cornell, C., & Gelles, R. (1982). Adolescent to parent violence. *Urban and Social Change Review*, 15: 8–14.

35. Cottrell, B., & Monk, P. (2004). Adolescent-to-parent abuse: A qualitative overview of common themes. *Journal of Family Issues*, 25: 1072–1095.

36. Ibid.

37. Brezina, T. (1999). Teenage violence toward parents as an adaptation to family strain: Evidence from a national survey of male adolescents. *Youth & Society*, 30: 416–444.

38. James, et al., 2000.

39. Wingood, G. M., DiClemente, R. J., Hubbard, D., McCree, K. H., and Davies, S. L. 2001. "Dating Violence and the Sexual Health of Black Adolescent Females." *Pediatrics*, 107.

40. Akers, R. 1985. *Deviant Behavior: A Social Learning Approach*. Belmont, CA: Wadsworth.

41. Miller et al. 2009.

42. Ibid.

43. Gray, H. M. and VangieFoshee, J. 1997. "Adolescent dating violence: differences between one-sided and mutually violent profiles." *Journal of Interpersonal Violence* 12(1): 126–142.

44. McCloskey, L. A. and. Lichter, E. L. 2003. "The Contribution of Marital Violence to Adolescent Aggression Across Different Relationships." *Journal of Interpersonal Violence* 18(4): 390–412.

45. Black, M. C., Noonan, R., Legg, M., Eaton, D., and Breiding, M. J. 2003. "Physical Dating Violence Among High School Students—United States, 2003" *MMWR Weekly*, 55(19): 532–535. Centers for Disease Control.

46. Hoffman, K., Kiecolt, K. J., and Edwards, J. N. 2005. "Physical Violence Between Siblings A Theoretical and Empirical Analysis" *Journal of Family Issues* November 2005, 26: 1103–1130.

47. Daly, K. and Chesney-Lind, M. 2003. "Feminism and Criminology." In Francis T. Cullen and Robert Agnew (Eds.), *Criminological Theory: Past to Present Essential Readings*. Los Angeles: Roxbury Publishing Company.

48. Goodwin, M. P. and Roscoe, B. 1990. "Sibling Violence and Agonistic Interactions Among Middle Adolescents." *Adolescence*. 25(98): 451–468.

49. Graham-Bermann S., Cutler, S. E., Litzenberger, B. W., and Schwartz, W. E. 1994. "Perceived Conflict and Violence in Childhood Sibling Relationships and other Emotional Adjustment." *Journal of Family Psychology,* 8(1): 85–97.

50. Hoffman, Kiecolt, and Edwards, 2005.

51. Agnew, R. S. 2003. "A General Strain Theory of Crime and Delinquency." In Francis T. Cullen and Robert Agnew (Eds.), *Criminological Theory: Past to Present Essential Readings.* Los Angeles: Roxbury Publishing Company.

52. Hardy, 2001.

53. Goodwin, M. P. and Roscoe, B. 1990. "Sibling Violence and Agonistic Interactions Among Middle Adolescents." *Adolescence.* 25(98): 451–468.

54. Hoffman, Kiecolt, and Edwards, 2005.

55. Peek, C. W., Fischer, J. L., and Kidwell, J. S. 1985. "Teenage Violence Towards Parents: A Neglected Dimension of Family Violence." *Journal of Family Violence.* 47, 1051–1058.

56. Ibid.

57. See for instance, Sherman, L. W. and Cohn, E. C. 1989. "The Impact of Research on Legal Policy: The Minneapolis Domestic Violence Experiment." *Law and Society Review* 23: 117–27.

58. Sherman, L. W., Smith, D. A., Schmidt, J. D., and Rogan, D. P. 1992. "Crime, Punishment, and Stake in Conformity: Legal and Informal Control of Domestic Violence." *American Sociological Review* 57: 680–690.

59. See for instance, http://www.law.jrank.org/pages/1548/Juvenile-Violent-Offenders-Causes-growth-decline-juvenile-violence.html.

60. http://www.cdc.gov/violenceprevention/pdf/IPV-SV_Program_Activities_Guide-a.pdf.

Chapter 6

Chronic Violent Juvenile Offenders

Case Studies in Delinquency

Clarence "Nightmare" Knight is a 17-year-old African American from Detroit, MI. He is a member of a local chapter of the Crips gang, and has a long association with the criminal justice system. Clarence has been arrested for aggravated assault, armed robbery, attempted murder of a police officer, conspiracy to traffic in narcotics, and a wide range of other crimes. Clarence has grown up institutionalized for most of his life. Coming from a large and chaotic family situation, which consisted of four boys and two girls, where Clarence was a "middle child," Clarence was often left on his own without adequate supervision. At age 12, Clarence was placed in foster care after being abused by his father and neglected by his mother. After running away from his foster family, state officials placed him in a detention center, where he quickly became involved in extortion and the assault of other youths. It was also in detention that Clarence joined a local chapter of the Crips, a nationally recognized violent gang. Upon his release, Clarence again ran away from his foster family and was arrested for a variety of other offenses, including assault, robbery, possession of narcotics, and burglary. After each episode officials began to notice that Clarence became more aggressive and he was not intimidated by the sanctions of the juvenile justice system. Consequently, officials became concerned that Clarence was becoming a violent and chronic offender who should be handled by the adult criminal justice system. Two months ago Clarence attempted to murder a rival gang member in a drive-by shooting. This time he was charged as an adult. He stated that no prison can hold him and nothing the state can do to him will cause him to change his ways. The prosecutor in the case is concerned because Clarence and other members of the Crips have a history of intimidating witnesses and victims, which results in their failure to testify against suspects.

Questions to Consider:

1. Is Clarence "salvageable" by the justice system or is he destined for a life of crime as an adult?
2. Should Clarence be tried as an adult or should some other type of intervention be used?
3. Can the juvenile justice system accommodate an offender like Clarence or is it really designed for the less violent offender?
4. How do offenders like Clarence impact community residents and shape their concerns and fears about violent crime?

They are perhaps the most feared of all young criminals: violent chronic offenders. These individuals, particularly if they are affiliated with a gang, are at the heart of the current policy debate concerning the future of the juvenile justice system and whether or not such individuals should be treated like adult criminals. It is this group that prompts policymakers, community activists, and politicians to reconsider the rehabilitative focus of the juvenile justice system and its ability to successfully reintegrate youths into society. To some extent, the public has a right to be concerned: one of the most important and consistent findings in the study of delinquency is that a small percentage of offenders are responsible for a large proportion of crime in the U.S.[1] The concept of a chronic offender is often used in the discussion of the career criminal, someone who has a long history of criminal activity lasting into adulthood. Unlike most youths who engage in delinquency and eventually stop, these individuals progress from delinquent activities to adult offenses and make crime a career.[2]

The concept of chronic offenders stems from a famous study conducted in Philadelphia by criminologists Marvin Wolfgang, Robert Figlio, and Terrence Sellin. These researchers examined the criminal careers of a group of boys born in Philadelphia in 1945 and followed them until they reached 18 years of age. The authors of the study gathered personal background, school-related information, and police records on 9,945 boys. The results showed that about 6% of the sample was made up of chronic offenders, meaning they had committed at least four criminal offenses.

This small group was responsible for more than half of the entire number of offenses that could be linked to the original 9,945 youths. Their acts were also quite serious: *the chronic 6%*, as they have now come to be called, accounted for 71% of the homicides, 73% of the forcible rapes, 82% of the robberies, and 69% of the aggravated assaults.[3] A second study was conducted by Wolfgang and his associates with similar results. In the second study, which was larger and included females, about 7.5% of the sample was responsible for most of the crime of that group.[4]

Other studies over time have shown that the chronic 6% are most likely to become adult offenders.[5] While much of the discussion of serious violent offenders focuses on the frequency and intensity of their crimes, their presence impacts almost every aspect of the criminal justice system. For example, police departments recognize the existence of chronic offenders and attempt to employ directed patrol strategies.[6] Repeat Offender Programs (ROP) are attempts to direct patrol efforts toward maximizing the opportunity to arrest chronic offenders.[7] Similarly, police/community programs such as *Weed and Seed* represent an effort to restore and revitalize disadvantaged neighborhoods and those touched by crime by "weeding" out the criminal element in a given community. This is done primarily by identifying chronic offenders and focusing a great deal of attention on their activities. Once the criminals are removed, residents and businesses can then "seed" the area with opportunities for growth and restoration.[8]

Similarly, mandatory sentences and automatic waiver laws for youths who commit serious crimes at age 16 or 17 are a direct result of the crimes committed by chronic and violent juvenile offenders. Finally, correctional institutions, which inherit these offenders for extended periods of time, are forced to address their violent criminal behavior along with their gang affiliations. The primary means to deal with such offenders is to segregate them from other gang members or from other inmates in general.

More recently, the research has shown this group to be a visible presence in the criminal landscape and official data continues to suggest that while violent and chronic juvenile offenders are the smallest group of delinquents in the United States, they play a significant role in the overall crime problem. For instance, African-American males under the age of 18 (the most common characteristics of chronic and violent juvenile offenders) constituted 51% of all juveniles arrested for homicide in 2008. Despite the fact that juvenile arrests for the most violent crimes have decreased since 1998, this group remains a significant feature of the offender landscape (see Table 6-1).

Table 6-1[9]
Ten-Year Trend of Arrests for Violent Crimes
by Suspects under Age 18
1998–2008

	1998	2008	% change
Violent Crime Arrests	58,886	53,819	−8.6%
Murder	735	670	−8.8%
Forcible Rape	2,539	1,848	−27.2%
Robbery	15,673	19,651	+25.4
Agg. Assault	39,939	31,650	−20.8%

As was mentioned, violent crime and gang-related activities are the two principal means by which juveniles threaten the public and generate a considerable sense of fear of victimization.

Juvenile Homicide

Despite the fact that the likelihood of such an event is actually low, many people are fearful of being a victim of a violent crime, particularly homicide. This does not mean, however, that there is no reason to be concerned about violent crime committed by youths. During the height of the crack-cocaine epidemic of the 1980s, for example, many youths fought for dominance in the drug marketplace. It was also during this time that a number of high-profile school shootings occurred, which added to the public's concern over youth violence. According to official statistics, the rate of juvenile arrests for homicide rose steadily in the 1980s before peaking in the early 1990s. However, in 1994 juvenile arrests began to decline sharply and have been fairly stable in recent years. Part of the explanation for this trend is that many of the turf battles over the drug markets have been resolved and youths involved in the trade have recognized that added attention from the police affects their overall profitability.

According to the FBI Uniform Crime Reports for 2009, arrests for homicides by juveniles are primarily a male phenomenon. That is, male juvenile arrests for homicide were nearly nine times greater than for females (8,755 vs. 1,020). Also noteworthy is the fact that African Americans are disproportionately represented in arrest statistics for juvenile homicide. While there are about as many whites as blacks arrested, there were more than twice as many Caucasians as African Americans in the U.S. population. This means that African Americans are arrested out of proportion to their population size. However, as with all official data, one must view these findings with caution as they only include offenses known to the police and reflect only those individuals who were arrested.[10]

A recent study by researchers at Northeastern University from 2002 to 2007, for example, showed that the number of homicides involving black juvenile males as offenders increased by 43% and as victims by nearly one-third. This increase in violence by youths is underscored by an increase in the number of gun-related homicides. Since 2000, the percentage of homicides involving a gun has increased for white and black offenders at all age categories.[11]

Some experts, noting the recent upswing in juvenile homicides, particularly among minority youth (where 85% of homicides involving African Americans are gun-related), suggest this increase relates to decreases in federal funding for the prevention of youth violence. Other experts note that many youths, even gang members, typically lack an important reference point of understanding of the short- and long-term impact of violence and homi-

cide. They claim that today's gang members were too young to remember the extensive gang-related violence of the early 1990s and
lack an appreciation for its consequences. For whatever reason,
there appears to be some inconsistency between reported homicide among youths and what is actually taking place.[12]

Gangs and Chronic Offending

A gang member may be one of the most enduring images people have when they think of delinquency. While the media por-
trayal of gangs tends to capitalize on the public's fears of
victimization, it is important to identify what is meant by the term
gang as well as understanding what kind of threat members pose to
a community. For example, if one were to simply follow the news
or claims made by politicians, it would appear that drive-by shootings and gang wars are common, gang members are violent, and
they are more likely to commit murder than ever before. However,
the most recent crime data from the Uniform Crime Reports in
2009 indicates that youths are responsible for only 15% of all violent crimes.[13] Additionally, consider the following statistics:
- A study from the Bureau of Justice Statistics shows that only
  10% of homicide convictions were under the age of 18.[14]
- The Uniform Crime Reports indicates that 5% of all homicides in 2009 were gang-related.[15]
- According to the National Youth Gang Survey, more than half
  of suburban areas and more than 75% of rural counties
  recorded no gang-related homicides in 2008.[16]

One of the more interesting aspects of the study of gangs is that
we may be seeing a significant shift in the way gangs operate, which
runs somewhat counter to gang affiliation in the first place. Traditionally, the bond that members had with each other was one of
the most important reasons for joining a gang. In fact, gang wars
are typically based on rivalries between gangs over turf or allegiance
to one group or another. Today researchers are witnessing a blur-
ring of those lines, which suggests that perhaps different reasons
for joining gangs may be emerging.

The term *gang* carries with it many meanings and evokes a number of different images for people. For some, a gang is a small group of four or five adolescents who loiter on a street corner. For others, the term may identify graffiti artists, drug users, Nazi Skinheads, or a group of highly organized youth whose purpose is to generate money from drug dealing. Defining a gang is difficult, and in order to find some type of working definition, we need to include a discussion of some of their different characteristics. In addition, the diversity in the perceptions of gangs, as well as how they are defined, presents specific challenges to communities as they attempt to deal with the problems in their particular neighborhoods. Many experts believe that the success or failure of community-wide attempts to address gangs is likely to rest in part on the way in which the problem is understood and diagnosed.[17]

There is also the problem of people affording responsibility for criminal behavior to gangs instead of to the individuals responsible. The term *gang-related* has become a marker to describe much of the crime that exists in many neighborhoods. However, the extent to which gangs are responsible for crime is often overstated. So how does one define a gang?

The media, the public, and community agencies use the term *gang* more loosely than the law enforcement community. People have come to believe that gangs are equated with highly organized drug distribution networks such as crack cocaine.[18] While drug use and selling has been a feature of gang life for many years, and some gangs are indeed involved in drug trafficking, the public's perception has become that all gangs are highly organized and heavily involved in the drug trade. Additionally, the drive-by shooting has become recognized as a popular characteristic of gang life.[19]

On the other hand, politicians and law enforcement officials tend to rely on legal parameters to define what constitutes a gang. However, these formal definitions often only reflect high-profile gangs or the ones that present the most pressing problems for police departments. Thus, from the law enforcement point of view, criminal behavior appears to be a key to the definition. For example, the Miami Police Department defines a gang as "a group of persons joined together to commit acts of violence or any other anti-social behavior."[20] The Los Angeles Police Department defines a gang as "a group of juveniles and/or adults in a geographic area whose activities include the unlawful use of force, violence, or threats of force and violence to further the group's purpose."[21] This is the most common definition used by police departments, but it fails to recognize the fact that many gangs do not engage solely in criminal acts, or even highly visible ones.

Even experts on gangs have great difficulty in reaching a consensus on an acceptable definition of a gang. Part of the problem is that there is a qualitative difference between a youth gang and a delinquent group—in the 1950s and 1960s, researchers viewed the delinquent gang and the delinquent group as identical. Today, however, when older adolescents and young adults are considered, researchers point out that distinctions need to be made. According to gang experts David Curry and Scott Decker, there are three criteria for defining a street gang:

- There is community recognition as a group or collectivity.
- Recognition by the group itself as a distinct group of either adolescents or young adults.
- Enough illegal activities to get a consistent negative response from law enforcement and/or neighborhood residents.[22]

However, even this definition presents problems since it implies a negative relationship between the community and the gang. Some gang experts have found that gangs often have a positive relationship with their local communities and often solve neighborhood problems informally.[23] Additionally, even though delinquents often commit illegal acts with others, sometimes referred to as *co-offending*, and even though co-offending is more common than solo acts of delinquency, these offenders do not necessarily constitute a gang.

One way to distinguish between the two is to compare *gang* behavior with *delinquent group* behavior. Research has shown that gang youths engage in quite a bit more criminal behavior: they have higher rates of police contact, more arrests, and more drug-related offenses.[24] Moreover, as youths mature they become less likely to engage in further criminal behavior,[25] but being a member of a gang decreases the likelihood that a youth will eventually stop committing crimes.

Another way to conceptualize gangs is to think of them as part of a larger continuum that represents how adolescents come together in groups. It is no secret that the teenage years are an important period in the lives of youths, and the groups they choose to connect with become critically important in terms of their social identities. But not all groups are bad for the youth's development (see Figure 6-1).

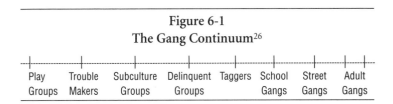

Figure 6-1
The Gang Continuum[26]

Gang expert James Howell describes the development of gangs on a continuum. On one end are simple play groups and at the other are criminal groups. Most youths affiliate with one or more of these types of groups during adolescence:

Childhood play groups. These are harmless groups of children that exist in every neighborhood.

Troublesome youth groups. This consists of youths who hang out together in shopping malls and other places to socialize. They may be involved in minor forms of delinquency, but usually they are typical teens who might get into trouble if the situation presents itself but usually do not.

Youth subculture groups. These are groups with special interests, who are not known for criminal involvement as a group even though some individuals may have been involved in criminal behavior. Examples include "Goths," named after the medieval Gothic period, who paint their faces pale-white, wear black clothing, and celebrate the death of things like dreams and hope and humanity for our culture. Another example would be "Geeks," who consist of intelligent students who are often social outcasts.

Delinquent groups. These groups consist of small clusters of friends who come together to commit delinquent acts such as vandalism, shoplifting, or burglary. Typically, these youths do not often socialize with each other beyond when they engage in delinquent acts. The defining feature of this group is the behavior its members engage in—minor forms of delinquency. **Taggers.** These groups come together for the purpose of painting graffiti in a wide range of locations within communities. Taggers, as we will see in the next chapter, are not violent and usually center their attention on artistic portrayals rather than crimes.

School-based youth gangs. This consists of groups of adolescents that may function as a gang only at school. While most members are not usually involved in delinquent activity when on school grounds, most members are involved in crime off-campus. The defining feature of this type of gang is the location in which their activities occur.

Street-based youth gangs. These are the more traditional types of gangs which can have loose affiliations with members and who engage in delinquent and criminal behavior.

Adult criminal organizations. This type of gang consists of groups of adults who engage in criminal activity primarily for economic reasons.[27]

As was mentioned, the term *gang-related* is often misused to describe the criminal activities of an individual member rather than the coordinated activities of the gang itself. In fact, the police often classify an incident as gang-related simply because the individual involved is a gang member. Gang experts Cheryl Maxson and Malcolm Klein refer to this as a *member-based definition*. Other departments may use a *motive-based definition* if the individual acts on behalf of the gang.[28] Still, it makes sense to separate the crimes a youth commits while acting as a gang member, such as assaulting rival gang members, from his or her own individual behavior, such as robbing a convenience store for personal gain. Unfortunately, the police tend to include most crimes committed by gang members as related to their membership in the organization.

In addition, many police departments have been confronted with another aspect of gang membership—youths who are on the fringes of gang membership, sometimes referred to as associates or "wanna-be" members. These youths hang around with full-fledged gang members but may not be recognized, either by the particular gang or by others, as a full and regular member of that gang. Determining if a youth is a member or a wanna-be is important since they often engage in very different types of activities. In fact, the distinction is so important that some departments require a youth to meet specific characteristics to be documented as a gang member. These include possession of gang tattoos, wearing gang colors, spraying gang graffiti, involvement in gang-related drive-bys, or commission of felonies with other gang members.[29]

Extent of Gangs

According to the National Youth Gang Survey (NYGS), which is an annual study of gangs and gang activity across the country, in the mid-1990s there was a significant decline in gang problems. This trend lasted until about 2001, and since then there has been a steady increase in gang activity. In 2007, overall there were an estimated 788,000 gang members and 27,000 active gangs in the United States. Rural counties have seen the most dramatic increase, even though gang activity is predominantly an urban phenomenon—between 2002 and 2007, the number of gang problems in rural areas increased by nearly 25%.[30]

Interestingly, adults make up the vast majority of gang members. According to the National Gang Center, in 2007, two-thirds of gang members were adults while only one-third consisted of juveniles. While the media appears to portray gang membership as a juvenile phenomenon, the data indicates that adults constitute the greatest proportion of gang members. Gangs that exist in rural areas or smaller cities tend to have a majority juvenile membership: according to the NYGS, approximately three-quarters of gang members in these locations are juveniles, while larger cities tend to attract adult members.[31]

According to the NYGS, larger cities have a much longer, more extensive history of gang problems—nearly half have experienced ongoing gang problems since before the 1990s. In contrast, very few rural counties have long-standing gang problems. In its 2007 report, the NYGS reported that an overwhelming majority of agencies noted a fluctuating trend of gang activity rather than a general increase. This trend is characterized by alternating periods of increasing and decreasing seriousness of the local gang problem.[32]

As was mentioned, there is a great deal of fluidity to gangs: they come in all shapes and sizes, come together for a variety of purposes, and often change their composition based on a number of factors. One of those factors is race and ethnicity. Most gangs are intra-racial, meaning that they tend to consist of members from similar race or ethnic backgrounds. Part of the reason for this stems from the geographic location in which gangs form. In some areas of Texas, for example, Hispanic gangs are much more prominent, largely because of the size of the Hispanic/Latino population in that area. In fact, according to the NYGS, Hispanic/Latinos make up about half of the gang members in the United States. About 35% of African Americans make up the total U.S. gang population, while whites represent about 9%. White ethnic groups, such as Italians, Irish, or even Jewish gangs, while popular at the turn of the century (when many white European immigrants came to this country), have, for the most part, assimilated into mainstream American culture. Thus, there are few white ethnic gangs in the U.S.[33] Having said that, white gangs are more likely to occur in rural areas than in large cities.[34]

Why Youths Join Gangs

Why do youths join gangs in the first place? What are the motivating factors that propel some youths to join a gang while others in the same neighborhood avoid a gang's influence? This is a difficult question to answer and while we cannot know for certain what motivates all youth in making that decision, some factors play a significant role in the process. According to the Los Angeles Police Department, youths join gangs for the following reasons:

- **Identity or Recognition.** Being part of a gang allows the gang member to achieve a level of status he or she feels impossible outside the gang culture.

- **Protection.** Many members join because they live in the gang area and are, therefore, subject to violence by rival gangs. Joining guarantees support in case of attack and retaliation for attacks.
- **Fellowship and Brotherhood.** To the majority of gang members, the gang functions as an extension of the family and may provide companionship lacking in the gang member's home environment. Many older brothers and relatives belong, or have belonged, to the gang. In addition, siblings who are members of gangs often socialize younger brothers into the gang life.
- **Intimidation.** Some members are forced to join if their membership will contribute to the gang's criminal activity. Some youths join gangs to intimidate residents in the community and other youths who are not involved in gang activity.
- **Criminal Activity.** Some join gangs in order to financially benefit from involvement in the drug trade and other crimes.[35]

According to one researcher's extensive work with gangs, which consisted of a 16-year-long study of high-risk youths in New York, two essential factors contribute to youths joining gangs. The first relates to stimulation. Youths who join gangs learn that drugs, girls, and excitement are associated with the gang. The second primary reason relates to survival. Many youths who join gangs realize that the only way to be protected from other gangs is to join one that can provide for their physical safety.

Other research on gang membership points to a variety of risk factors that place adolescents at an increased risk for joining a gang. Those factors include the following:

- Early involvement in delinquency, especially with violence and drug use.
- Troubled family relationships.
- Low attachment to school and poor grades.
- Association with youth involved with gangs, including older siblings.
- Living in neighborhoods with gangs.[36]

The greater the number of these factors that exists in a child's life, the greater the likelihood that he or she will join a gang. Hanging out with delinquent peers, school failure at the elementary level, and sexual activity at an early age are among the stronger predictors of gang membership.[37] While gang members are more likely than other delinquents to become chronic adult offenders, most gang members eventually leave their gang.[38] This *aging out* process, where a youth matures and finds other activities that take priority over the gang, is common among all youth, including most delinquents. As they get older, most gang members get married, find legitimate jobs, and settle down.[39]

Case Studies in Delinquency
Clarence "Nightmare" Knight

Given what you have read thus far about family structure, gangs, and violence, what do we make of Clarence's situation? Is it the case that he is a wayward youth who, with some treatment and assistance, can become a productive member of society, or is he simply too far along in his criminal career to be salvaged? What can be done to bring Clarence closer to conformity and constructive behavior? Or should we simply treat him as an adult and accept the fact that he will likely become a chronic adult offender?

The Changing Nature of Gangs

More recently, the study of gangs has taken on new dimensions. In fact, some evidence shows that many of the reasons for joining a gang: the sense of belonging, the pseudo-family structure, loyalty to one's in-group, as well as social cohesion among its members, are changing. Some evidence exists of what are called *hybrid gangs*, which consist of members of different gangs that come together for a particular activity, such as the drug trade. This has occurred in the past, but experts are witnessing instances in which rival gang members, even arch rivals such as Bloods and Crips, are interacting and working together in various ways. Thus, perhaps we are seeing a breakdown of the boundaries that traditionally have segregated gangs and created hostilities and rivalries between them.[40]

Hybrid gangs became a part of the gang landscape in the mid-1980s and 1990s as gang migration patterns emerged. Gang migration is simply the movement of gang members from one region of the country to another. With this physical relocation, the traditional understanding and parameters of gang structure began to change. While some experts contend that hybrid gangs have existed since the 1920s, they became more pronounced within the last twenty years.[41] Part of the challenge for law enforcement with regard to hybrid gangs was that much of the training that existed on gangs became obsolete: identifiers, patterns, and trends that used to assist the police in identifying and suppressing gang activities no longer applied to hybrid gangs.

According to a report by the Bureau of Justice Statistics, Kansas City, MO was one of the first cities to experience gang migration. In the early 1980s Kansas City began to see a flood of gang members from Los Angeles-affiliated gangs into the area, such as Crips and Bloods, who became immersed in the drug trade there. This was followed by the presence of Chicago-based gang members a short time later. Other cities in the Midwest began to experience a gang presence as well. The difference, of course, is that members were not simply transferring a typical structure of the gang found at its home base, but members began to blur the lines between rival gangs.[42]

For example, hybrid gangs may or may not have an allegiance to a traditional gang color. In fact, much of the hybrid gang graffiti in the United States is a composite of multiple gangs with conflicting symbols. For example, Crips gang graffiti painted in red (the color used by the rival Blood gang) would be unheard of in California but has occurred elsewhere in the hybrid gang culture.[43]

Gang members may also change their affiliation from one gang to another. It is not uncommon for a gang member to claim multiple affiliations, sometimes with rival gangs. For example, the police may encounter an admitted Blood gang member who is also known in another city as a member of the Black Gangster Disciples gang. Existing gangs may even change their names or suddenly merge with other gangs to form new ones. Although many gangs continue to be based on race and ethnicity, many are increasingly diverse in terms of race, ethnicity and gender. Hybrid gangs can also be homegrown and consider themselves to be distinct entities with no alliance to groups such as the Bloods/Crips or Folk/People.[44]

Another change in the nature of gangs is their involvement in the military. In a 2009 report entitled *Gang Activity in the U.S. Armed Forces Increasing*, the FBI states that members of nearly every major street gang, including the Bloods, Crips, Gangster Disciples, Hells Angels, Latin Kings, Mara Salvatrucha (MS-13), Mexican Mafia, Vice Lords, and various White supremacist groups, have been documented on military installations. Although most prevalent in the Army, the Army Reserves, and the National Guard, gang activity is pervasive throughout all branches of the military and across most ranks. However, the report suggests that gang membership appears to cluster among the junior enlisted ranks.[45]

Additionally, the extent of gang presence in the military is often difficult to determine since many gang members conceal their gang affiliation and military authorities may not recognize gang characteristics. In addition, the military is also not required to report criminal offense statistics occurring on installations to the FBI, nor is it likely to do so if such a situation reflects poorly on that particular branch of the service.

Part of the explanation for this trend relates to training: some gang members enlist in the military to receive weapons and combat training. Once they are discharged, gang members can then employ their skills against law enforcement officials and rival gang members. An added layer to the prevalence of gang members in the military is the tendency for criminal courts to allow gang members to enlist in lieu of a prison sentence. While this practice violates military recruiting regulations, a gang member facing criminal charges may be given the option to join the military or serve a jail sentence. Part of the reason for this strategy stems from the overcrowding that exists in many U.S. prisons, making military service a reasonable alternative in the minds of many judges. The problem, however, is that once these individuals receive combat training, not to mention access to weapons and explosives, the threat they pose to the community upon their return is considerable. In addition, since most gang members maintain an allegiance to their gang while serving in the military, the safety of other soldiers and commanding officers is jeopardized. More globally, gang rivalries within the military could also compromise its ability to complete its objectives in places like Iraq and Afghanistan.[46]

This expansion of the gang problem to other areas across the country has led to a debate about why it is occurring. Some experts believe, for example, that the migration of gang members reflects the corporate expansion of gangs and their criminal activities. Similar to businesses that expand once they begin to prosper, this school of thought suggests that gangs are tapping into areas traditionally insulated from gang-related criminal activities.[47] In contrast, other experts claim that the increase in the number of communities reporting gang problems reflects either the changing definitions of gangs or perhaps the movement of youths from one part of the country to another for reasons other than gang expansion. For example, a gang member's family may relocate to a new location, resulting in their developing gang activities, but the reason for the relocation was not related to gang membership.[48]

Explaining Chronic Violent Offenders

Violent juvenile offenders tend to have a history of truancy and dropping out, substance abuse problems, as well as mental health issues. Violent offenders also tend to begin their criminal careers at a young age and continue this pattern into adulthood. Some evidence suggests that this population is getting younger, with some children as young as ten years old becoming involved in violent crime. It was this group, too, that became the basis for the prediction in the 1990s of the aforementioned "super predator" category of delinquents. The spotlight on this segment of the delinquent population was due in part to the increases in crime and arrest statistics, but also to the aforementioned social distortion of delinquency by the media.

Recall that the leading proponents of this prediction were professors John DiLuilio of Princeton University and James Fox of Northeastern University. Juvenile super predators were described as sociopaths with no moral conscience who see crime as a rite of passage. They were also described as youths who were not deterred by the sanctions that could be leveled against them by the juvenile justice system.[49]

The argument presented by advocates of this position was that violent juvenile crime was increasing and would continue to increase because this small group of juvenile super predators committed more crimes more frequently than delinquents of past generations. The supporters of this argument also concluded that this new breed of delinquent would not be affected by the rehabilitative approach of the juvenile justice system. Because this cohort of disturbed youths was so violent and irrational, the only reasonable solution would be to increase punitive sanctions and to treat them as the violent future adults they would eventually become.[50]

In response to this growing "threat" of offender, and the subsequent fear it generated for policymakers, nearly every state in the early 1990s changed how their justice systems responded to violent juveniles. These changes were all designed to increase the flow of juveniles into the adult criminal justice system.[51] While this prediction of a super predator failed to materialize, the concern about violent juvenile offenders remains high and many of the policies and laws enacted have remained in effect.

Treating Chronic Violent Offenders

The most significant and expensive outcome of a court referral for juveniles is residential placement, such as a detention center, a wilderness program, a treatment center or a group home. In 2007, there were approximately 160,000 juvenile offenders placed in one of these types of facilities. The best available data on the length of stay for all juveniles in residential placement is about four months, although the length of stay depends on the seriousness of the offense. Crimes against persons were committed by about 35% of placed offenders, while about 20% had committed a violation of their probation or parole agreement (such as not attending school, missing curfew, or a failed drug test).

Given the expense and harm associated with these types of offenders, and given the wide range of placements available, a reasonable question would be to determine which ones are the most effective in changing youths' behavior. A review of a number of reports outlining the overall effectiveness of these types of programs, such as the Blueprints for Violence Prevention series, the Surgeon General's report on youth violence, as well as a number of meta-analyses of studies conducted on these programs, reveals several identifiable trends. This review is particularly important and relevant given the "get tough" approach that has been influencing the operation of the juvenile justice system in recent years.

In the content of these reports and discussions, five major strategies were assessed in terms of their ability to reduce reoffending behavior by violent juvenile offenders. These strategies include formal processing by the juvenile justice system; the use of waiver laws that allow juveniles to be treated like adults in the justice system; surveillance, which primarily includes probation and parole; shock incarceration, such as the "scared straight" approach, in which youths are brought to adult prisons and intimidated into conformity; and residential placement, which includes formal detention/incarceration.

Formal Processing Instead of Handling Cases Informally

While juvenile justice officials prefer to handle most cases informally, and while it is true that diversion can occur at any stage of the process, an increasingly popular sentiment exists that the juvenile justice system has gone "soft" on offenders. This means that the current justice model does not deter offenders from committing additional crimes, as evidenced by a high recidivism (re-arrest) rate. Such a finding is often used as a justification for formally processing more juveniles and for referring many cases for adjudication or trial. However, in one of the most extensive meta-analyses on the value of court processing as a way to deter future crimes, the authors noted that, when compared to the use of community services, formally charging and adjudicating youths tended to increase criminal behavior rather than deter it. This means that formal processing actually increases the likelihood that a youth will commit another criminal act.[52]

Juvenile Waiver Laws

Another popular method of handling juveniles is to treat them similarly as adults. All states have some type of mechanism for handling juveniles in criminal court, and some states have even passed statutes that mandate automatic waiver if the youth in question is of a certain age (often 16 or 17 years old). Juvenile waivers are based on the philosophical idea that if a youth commits an adult crime, they should be punished as if he or she were an adult. Similar to formal processing by the juvenile court, such an approach is said to deter youths from committing crimes since the punishment outweighs the benefits. However, a review of the literature suggests that not only are a small percentage of youths waived to adult court, but when compared to youths adjudicated in juvenile court, transfer to adult criminal court is associated with *higher* recidivism rates. This relationship holds true whether it involves juveniles convicted of property or person offenses. Thus, like formal processing in general, waivers to adult court actually increase the likelihood of criminal behavior by delinquent youths rather than reducing it.[53]

Intensive Surveillance

One of the most common dispositions for juveniles who are processed through the juvenile justice system involves probation, a mechanism that involves supervision of youths for a period of time as a condition of their release.[54] Further, youths who have been released from detention are often placed on parole, sometimes called *intensive probation*, which is a type of close surveillance until their sentence has been completed. Given that judges make use of probation in the vast majority of cases, one has to wonder about the impact such supervision has on recidivism. In general, the evidence on the effectiveness is mixed. One study that involved a meta-analysis found no effect,[55] while others found only a small impact on offenders.[56] Still another study found that intensive supervision could be effective if it is part of a larger overall therapeutic treatment program, but by itself, it does not reduce recidivism.[57]

Shock Incarceration

Another program, "Scared Straight," brought youths who were on probation into maximum-security prisons to interact with adult prisoners. The original Scared Straight program began in the 1970s. Inmates serving life sentences at Rahway State Prison in New Jersey began a program in which they would "scare" at-risk or delinquent children using an aggressive depiction of the violence that permeates social life in prison. This original program generated media attention and a television documentary touting a 94% success rate. Subsequent programs modeled after Scared Straight reported success rates between 80% and 90%.[58]

While popular with politicians, policymakers, and even declared successful by many practitioners, one evaluation of Scared Straight programs showed that participants were actually more likely to be arrested than non-participants.[59] To underscore this initial finding, a rigorous review of Scared Straight programs was conducted in 2002. From the 500 available articles and studies of such programs in the literature, nine studies met complicated methodological criteria to ensure the program and its evaluation were conducted properly. The focus of investigation was on the proportion of each group (Scared Straight or control) that committed additional crimes. The results showed that the youths who went through the Scared Straight programs had higher recidivism rates than those youths who did not go through the program.[60] In the end, the research shows that these types of interventions result in increased criminal activity for juvenile offenders compared to those who do not participate in them.

Residential Placement

The goal of residential placement is to provide youths with the proper environment in which to receive treatment. This is particularly true for youths who come to residential placement after other alternatives have failed. These particular youths bring with them a host of issues and problems, including substance abuse, mental health issues, and a lack of educational achievement. The goal of residential programs is to take youths out of crime-producing environments and provide intensive forms of therapy in the hope of reducing recidivism. However, like the other programs, as a general rule residential placement has not been successful in curtailing or reducing delinquency. In fact, the empirical literature suggests that bringing together youths with these types of issues and backgrounds, especially for extended periods of time, only provides greater opportunities for further delinquency and increases the likelihood of recidivism.[61]

Effective Programs
for Violent Juvenile Offenders

While it seems fairly clear that there are a variety of programs that are ineffective in reducing recidivism among this segment of the population, researchers have also identified which programs are effective and the key components to successful interventions. These include the following four general principles:

1. Targeting the risk factors that relate to offending.
2. Programs should focus on interventions that are behavioral in nature.
3. Programs should be individualized to the strengths and weaknesses of the offender.
4. Interventions should primarily target high-risk offenders.[62]

These general principles are supported by other research that establishes a clear pattern of the types of programs that are effective in reducing recidivism among violent and chronic juvenile offenders. Unfortunately, these programs only target approximately 15,000 youths in the United States, a rather small number when compared to the 160,000 who are placed in residential treatment each year.[63]

Summary

Clearly, much of the concern about juvenile crime, and to a great extent the changes in the juvenile justice system, have come as a result of concerns about violent offenders. The public's image of juvenile crime in general stems from sensational media accounts of violent gang members engaging in extreme forms of violence against other gangs as well as the public. Given that public policy is often shaped by what is perceived to be the cause of the problem, the recent philosophy witnessed in the juvenile justice system comes largely from the perception that chronic and violent individuals make up the bulk of the juvenile offender population. The highlight of this trend was the prediction of a super predator class of delinquents, which led policy makers to focus attention away from the factors that contributed to violence and more on punishing the individual. The impact of this trend was also seen in the increases in the number and size of prisons and the decline of federal funding for delinquency prevention and rehabilitation programs, despite the fact that there is a considerable amount of evidence that detention and incarceration are ineffective methods to reduce recidivism.[64]

Notes

1. See DeLisi, M. 2005. *Career Criminals in Society.* Belmont, CA: Sage.

2. Ibid.

3. Wolfgang, M. E., Figlio, R. M., and Sellin, T. 1972. *Delinquency in a Birth Cohort.* Chicago: University of Chicago Press.

4. Wolfgang, M. E., Thornberry, T. P., Figlio, R. M. 1987. *From Boys to Men, From Delinquency to Crime.* Chicago, University of Chicago Press.

5. See Howell, J. C. 1995. *Guide for Implementing the Comprehensive Strategy for Serious, Violent, and Chronic Juvenile Offenders.* Washington, DC: National Institute of Justice, Office of Juvenile Justice and Delinquency Prevention.

6. Kappeler, V. 2005. *Policing in America.* 5th edition. Belmont, CA: Wadsworth.

7. Ibid.

8. See U.S. Department of Justice, Office of Justice Programs, Community Capacity Development Office, Executive Office of Weed and Seed. http://www.ojp.usdoj.gov/ccdo/ws/welcome.html accessed August 11, 2008.

9. Source: *Crime in the United States 2009* Available at http://www.fbi.gov/ucr/cius2008/data/table_32.html.

10. Ibid.

11. Fox, J. A. and Swatt, M. 2008. *Recent Surge in Homicides Involving Young Black Males and Guns: Time To Reinvest in Prevention and Crime Control.* Boston, MA: Northeastern University.

12. Ibid.

13. U.S. Department of Justice, Federal Bureau of Investigation, 2006. *Crime in the United States, 2005.* Table 9: Expanded Homicide Data. Washington, DC: U.S. Government Printing Office.

14. Catalano, S. M. 2006. *Criminal Victimization, 2005.* Washington, DC: Bureau of Justice Statistics.

15. Department of Justice, Federal Bureau of Investigation. 2009. Expanded Homicide Index. http://www2.fbi.gov/ucr/cius2009/offenses/expanded_information/data/shrtable_12.html.

16. U.S. Department of Justice, Federal Bureau of Investigation. 2009. *Crime in the United States.* Washington, DC: U.S. Government Printing Office. Accessed at http://www.fbi.gov/ucr/ucr.htm.

17. Steadman, J. and Weisel, D. 1998. *Addressing Community Gang Problems: A Practical Guide.* U.S. Department of Justice, Office of Justice Programs, Bureau of Justice Assistance.

18. Fagan, J. 1993. "The Political Economy of Drug Dealing Among Urban Gangs" in *Drugs and Community*. Davis, R.C., Lurigio, A. and Rosenbaum, D. (eds.). Chicago: University of Chicago Press.

19. See for instance Sanders, W. 1994. *Gangbangs, and Drive-bys: Grounded Culture and Juvenile Gang Violence*. New York: Aldine de Gruyter.

20. See http://www.miami-police.org/dept/overview.asp?dept=Juvenile.

21. See http://www.lapdonline.org/search_results/content_basic_view/1396.

22. Curry, G. D. and Decker, S. H. 1998. *Confronting Gangs: Crime and Community*. Los Angeles: Roxbury.

23. Jankowski, M. 1991. *Islands in the Street: Gangs and American Urban Society*. Berkeley, CA: University of California Press.

24. See Klein, M. W. and Maxson, C. L. 2001. *Gang Structures, Crime Patterns, and Police Responses: A Summary Report*. Washington, DC: Office of Juvenile Justice and Delinquency Prevention. Available at: http://www.ncjrs.gov/pdffiles1/nij/grants/188510.pdf.

25. See for instance, Hoge, R. 2001. *The Juvenile Offender: Theory, Research, and Application*. New York: Springer.

26. Adapted from Howell, J. C. 2003. *Preventing & Reducing Juvenile Delinquency: A Comprehensive Framework*. Thousand Oaks, CA: Sage Publications.

27. Howell, J. C. 2003. *Preventing & Reducing Juvenile Delinquency: A Comprehensive Framework*. Thousand Oaks, CA: Sage Publications.

28. Maxon, C. and M. Klein. 2001. "Street Gang Violence: Twice as Great or Half as Great" in *Gangs in America*. C. Ron Huff (ed.). Newbury Park, CA: Sage, pp.71–102.

29. Katz, C. 2003. "Issues in the Production and Dissemination of Gang Statistics: An Ethnographic Study of a Large Midwestern Police Gang Unit." *Crime and Delinquency*, 49: 406.

30. Department of Justice, Office of Justice Programs, Office of Juvenile Justice and Delinquency Prevention. 2009. *Highlights of the 2007 National Gang Youth Survey*. http://www.iir.com/NYGC/

publications/2007-survey-highlights.pdf.
    31. Ibid. See also National Gang Center http://www.national-gangcenter.gov/Survey-Analysis/Gang-Related-Offenses.
    32. U.S. Department of Justice, Office of Justice Programs, Office of Juvenile Justice and Delinquency Prevention. 2009. *National Youth Gang Survey Report.* Tallahassee, FL: Institute for Intergovernmental Research.
    33. Ibid.
    34. Office of Juvenile Justice and Delinquency Prevention. 2009. *National Youth Gang Survey Report.*
    35. See LAPD Gang Unit website at http://www.lapdonline.org/search_results/content_basic_view/1396.
    36. Thornberry, T. P. and Krohn, M. D. 2003. (eds), *Taking Stock of Delinquency: An Overview of Findings from Contemporary Longitudinal Studies.* New York: Kluwer.
    37. Ibid.
    38. Delaney, 2006.
    39. Ibid.
    40. Starbuck, D., Howell, J. C., and Lindquist, D. J. 2001 *Hybrid and Other Modern Gangs.* Washington DC: Office of Juvenile Justice Delinquency Prevention. See also Miller, M.; Ventura, H.; and Tatum, J. 2004. "An Assessment of Gang Presence and Related Activities at the County Level: Another Deniability Refutation." *Journal of Gang Research*, 11(2): 1–22.
    41. Ibid.
    42. Miller, Ventura and Tatum, 2004.
    43. Starbuck, Howell, and Lindquist. 2001.
    44. Ibid.
    45. FBI 2009 report entitled *Gang Activity in the U.S. Armed Forces Increasing* 46. http://usmilitary.about.com/od/justicelaw legislation/a/gangs.htm.
    47. Shelden, Tracy, and Brown, 2004.
    48. Ibid.
    49. Juvenile Violent Offenders—The Concept Of The Juvenile Super Predator http://law.jrank.org/pages/1546/Juvenile-Violent-Offenders-concept-juvenile-super-predator.html#ixzz0auiTs8YR.
    50. Ibid.

51. Ibid.

52. See Petrosino, A., Turpin-Petrosino, C., and Guckenburg, S. 2010. *Formal System Processing of Juveniles: Effects on Delinquency.* Los Angeles, CA: Campbell Systematic Reviews.

53. Redding, R. E. 2010. *Juvenile Justice Bulletin: Juvenile Transfer Laws: An Effective Deterrent to Delinquency?* Washington, DC: Office of Juvenile Justice and Delinquency Prevention.

54. Snyder, H. N. and Sickmund, M. 2006. *Juvenile Offenders and Victims: A 2006 National Report.* Washington, DC: U.S. Department of Justice, Office of Justice Programs, Office of Juvenile Justice and Delinquency Prevention. Available at http://www.ojjdp. gov/ojstatbb/nr2006/downloads/nr2006.pdf.

55. Drake, E. K., Aos, S., and Miller, M. G. 2009. "Evidence-based Public Policy Options to Reduce Crime and Criminal Justice Costs: Implications in Washington State." *Victims and Offenders,* 4, 170–196.

56. Lipsey, M. W. 2009. "The Primary Factors that Characterize Effective Interventions with Juvenile Offenders: a Meta-analytic Overview." *Victims and Offenders,* 4: 124–147.

57. Howell, J. C. 2003. *Preventing and Reducing Juvenile Delinquency: A Comprehensive Framework.* Thousand Oaks, CA: Sage.

58. Finckenauer, J. O. 1982. *Scared Straight and the Panacea Phenomenon.* Englewood Cliffs, NJ: Prentice Hall.; Petrosino, A., Turpin-Petrosino, C., and Buehler, J. 2003. "Scared Straight" and other juvenile awareness programs for preventing juvenile delinquency" In: *The Campbell Collaborative Reviews Of Intervention and Policy Evaluations (C2-RIPE).* Philadelphia, PA: Campbell Collaboration.

59. Ibid.

60. Petrosino, A., Turpin-Petrosino, C., Buehler, J. 2003. "Scared Straight and Other Juvenile Awareness Programs for Preventing Juvenile Delinquency: A Systematic Review of the Randomized Experimental Evidence." The ANNALS of the American Academy of Political and Social Science 589: 41 62.

61. See for instance, Dodge, K. A., Dishion, T. J., and Lansford, J. E. 2006. *Deviant Peer Influences in Programs for Youth: Problems and Solutions.* New York: Guilford Press. See also Sedlak, A. J. and McPherson, K. S. 2010. Juvenile Justice Bulletin: *Conditions of Con-*

finement: Findings from the Survey of Youth in Residential Placement. Washington, DC: U.S. Department of Justice, Office of Justice Programs, Office of Juvenile Justice and Delinquency Prevention.

62. See for instance Howell, 2003. See also, Cullen, F. T., Myer, A. J., and Latessa, E. J. 2009. "Eight Lessons from Moneyball: The High Cost of Ignoring Evidence-based Corrections." *Victims and Offenders,* 4: 197–213.

63. Puzzanchera, C. and Kang, W. 2010. *Easy Access to Juvenile Court Statistics. 1985–2007.* Washington, DC: Office Of Juvenile Justice and Delinquency Prevention. Available at http://ojjdp.ncjrs.gov/ojstatbb/ezajsc.

64. Ibid.

Chapter 7

Non-Violent Chronic Offenders

Case Studies in Delinquency

Adam Zaleski, also known as Baby Z, is a fifteen-year-old from Chicago, Illinois. He and his parents recently moved to a rural town in Georgia when his father, who serves in the military, was transferred. Adam is an artistic young man, who sketches, paints, and creates sculptures out of wood and stone. Adam quickly made friends at his local high school and began creating murals and other paintings on public walls around town. Many of the buildings on which he spray painted his name or some other creation were old, in need of repair, and contributed to the decline of the use of the downtown area by residents. The primary reason for this was that many people who lived in this small town preferred to drive thirty minutes to a larger city nearby to take advantage of the wider selection of shops, restaurants, movie theaters and other activities. Adam was eventually caught by the local police for tagging the buildings. When he was brought before a juvenile court judge, Adam could not be convinced of the inappropriateness of his acts. He continued to proclaim that he was actually making a contribution to the community by improving the overall look of the downtown area. Since his tagging did not consist of gang symbols or offensive remarks, Adam believed he was improving the aesthetics of the neighborhood. This was particularly true since many of the buildings had not been renovated in some time and the owners did not seem to be interested in remodeling or improving their physical appearance.

Questions to Consider:
1. Has Baby Z committed a crime? If so which one(s)?
2. What do you think the judge will say in response to Baby Z's assertion that his work should be considered art rather than vandalism?
3. What do you think the community's reaction will be, if any? Should they care given that most of them do not use the downtown area anyway?

In the last chapter, we discussed chronic juvenile offenders who engage in a variety of violent acts. In this chapter the focus is on those individuals who, while non-violent and do not necessarily pose a physical threat to the public, engage in a variety of behaviors that are costly, chronic, and criminal in nature. These include computer hacking, vandalism (which includes graffiti), and status offenses, such as underage drinking and smoking.

Computer Hacking

Recent research on computer "hacking" makes explicit reference to the disproportionate involvement of juveniles in this form of computer crime. While hacking is not a typical topic for researchers who study delinquency, the available evidence suggests that it should be based on how many youths are involved.[1] A hacker may be defined as a "person who enjoys learning the details of computer systems and how to stretch their capabilities or one who programs enthusiastically or who enjoys programming rather than just theorizing about programming."[2]

There are actually several different types or frameworks to understand hacking. *Cracking,* a term used to describe the tendency for hackers to break into secure databases, can also be understood on a continuum of motives, where some do it for the challenge while others do it to for "ethical" reasons, such as to point out the vulnerabilities of a database or agency.[3]

Experts on computer crime believe that hacking began with the creation of the interstate phone system and direct long-distance dialing in the late 1950s. The switching devices used to make the connections between phones were easily duplicated and *phone phreaking*, where calls are made without paying the appropriate fee, began.[4] Early hackers were also able to create phone numbers that would never be billed for service. With the advent of cellular phones, hackers began to use a combination of cellular and landline phones to prevent the police from tracking them.[5]

While the types and methods used to hack into computers is virtually limitless, according to some experts, there are three common methods hackers use to gain access to a computer and steal information. *Spoofing* is the process by which a hacker gains access by pretending to be a legitimate user. The rationale behind the success of spoofing is based on the idea that computer security systems perform only limited checks to ascertain the identity of a user at the login phase. Therefore, by feeding a minimal amount of information to the computer, a hacker can pose as a valid user.

Another method by which a hacker can spoof is called *Social Engineering*. In this case, a hacker persuades a legitimate user to reveal computer access information by pretending to be a user having trouble accessing the system, such as saying they lost their login information. Finally, hackers can get information relating to legitimate users' access information by *Dumpster Diving*. By searching through a company's trash, hackers can acquire login names and passwords and access telephone numbers and other confidential information about the company's computer system.[6]

Explaining Computer Hacking

Understanding hacking is complicated, in part because there is no single type of hacker, and like other offenders discussed in this chapter, little empirical information is available on this population. In one of the few sociological studies of its kind, criminologist Robert Taylor developed a profile of the juvenile hacker based on data available from 100 convicted juvenile hackers. The typical hacker is a white male, between the ages of 14 and 20, from middle- to upper-class backgrounds, with intact and stable families. Hackers tend to be loners, although they do have a wide assortment of friends via the Internet, especially other hackers. This virtual relationship is important as it provides insight, advice, status, and emotional support. Taylor found that typical hackers are highly intelligent and creative, although socially they feel most comfortable with other hackers—and even then, only in certain situations, such as online. Despite high levels of intelligence, hackers tend to be underachievers at school, likely because of boredom or feeling uncomfortable in situations involving interaction with others.[7]

Other experts focus on the psychology of hacking: they argue that these offenders are emotionally insecure and hacking allows them to feel as though they are in control of their world. The competition with other hackers, including attempts to upstage each other, gives them a way to feel good about themselves.[8] Still other experts take a more holistic view of hacking and explain it as a modern-day boyhood ritual, where adolescents explore areas that are off limits and forbidden simply to test the boundaries of appropriate behavior. In these situations, computer hacking is simply the latest version of mischief with a technological twist.[9]

One way to understand hacking is by examining the motives behind the behavior. The following typology provides a better grasp of the intent of hackers.

- **Visionaries.** These individuals are not necessarily hard-core criminals as much as they are fascinated with the ways in which technology can affect society.
- **Kickers.** These are hackers who do not intend to inflict harm on any individual or society, rather they are in it for the thrill and fun of hacking.
- **Adventurers.** This category consists of hackers who break into computer systems for the challenge and sense of adventure it presents.
- **Gamers.** These types of hackers focus primarily on defeating the software protection on computer games. Defeating the software engineers who create programs to thwart hacking becomes a source of status and prestige for these types of offenders.
- **Destroyers.** This type of hacker focuses on malicious and intentional destruction of other people's property—there is no apparent constructive gain involved.[10]

Thus, while some hackers are motivated by financial gain, other motives include thrill and excitement (similar to joyriding for motor vehicle theft or shoplifting just for the fun of it), or as a passive/aggressive reaction to society's status quo.[11]

One of the most famous computer hackers in the U.S. was Kevin David Mitnick. Beginning his hacking career in suburban Los Angeles in the mid-1970s, Mitnick stole service from Pacific Bell's telephone system. In 1981 Mitnick and two friends broke into the Pacific Bell phone center in downtown Los Angeles. Eventually, Mitnick was arrested; however, because he was only a minor, he was treated as a delinquent instead of an adult criminal.[12]

In 1983, Mitnick was arrested by the campus police of the University of Southern California for using a university computer to hack into the ARPANET, the military version of the Internet at the time. As a result of this offense, Mitnick served six months in a juvenile prison.[13]

In 1988, Mitnick gained national attention after he and a friend hacked into the computers of Digital Equipment Corporation (DEC). Mitnick was caught and argued that he was psychologically addicted to hacking. A plea bargain sent Mitnick to prison for one year and then to counseling for six months.

After his release, Mitnick continued hacking until his arrest in 1995.[14] Upon his release from prison, Mitnick created a security firm that, somewhat ironically, provides computer consulting to stop hackers. He has written two books entitled *The Art of Intrusion*, a book on computer hacking, and *The Art of Deception*, a book focusing on personal security.[15]

The threats posed by computer hacking are serious and present numerous problems for society. While some hackers are only engaging in minor crimes, others have more ambitious goals. In 2009, McAfee security software president Dave Dewalt said, "Last year we saw a 500% increase in malware ... malicious software like worms or viruses. That was more than we saw in the last five years combined."[16] So dangerous is the threat of cybercrime that it has become a priority during President Obama's administration. In 2009 he created a new position of "Cyber Czar" to protect the nation's computer networks. Citing the risks to citizens' information, money, as well as the potential threats of Al Qaeda and other terrorist groups who have threatened cyber attacks on the U.S., President Obama has made cybercrime and hackers a priority.[17]

As it relates to juvenile justice, while there may be a tendency to treat hacking as an episode of youthful mischief, most hackers begin as juveniles and progress into adult offenders. This makes the challenge for juvenile justice officials a significant one since the behavior is not likely to end once the youth reaches a certain age. However, more severe punishments run counter to the treatment-orientation of the juvenile justice system, particularly since these offenders are non-violent. However, the risks they pose to society are formidable.

Recent Trends: Ethical Hacking

Ethical hacking, which is sometimes known as *penetration testing*, has gained some recent notoriety. Organizations are increasingly evaluating the success or failure of their current security measures through the use of ethical hacking processes. According to some, "Ethical hacking may be one of the most effective ways to proactively plug rampant security holes."[18] Moreover, many security experts encourage organizations to hire ethical hackers to test their networks.[19]

According to those within the security field, an increased number of information technology professionals are going back to class to learn the latest hacking techniques. In fact, many consider the three- to five-day seminars to be less expensive than hiring outside consultants or the organizational costs of being hacked. The average cost for the seminars is between $2,000 to $8,000 per person, while consulting services range from $10,000 to $100,000.[20]

According to the 2005 Computer Crime and Security Survey, virus attacks continue to be the source of greatest financial loss for most organizations. Unauthorized use has increased as has unauthorized access to information and theft of proprietary information. All of these increase the average dollar loss per respondent.[21]

Vandalism

One of the most common crimes committed by youths, aside from larceny, is vandalism. While there are a host of activities that can be classified as vandalism, by definition it consists of activities that involve the deliberate, mischievous, or malicious destruction or damage of property.[22] According to the Uniform Crime Reports, there were approximately 212,981 arrests for vandalism in 2009, of which 71,502 were of individuals under age 18.

Table 7-1[23]
Uniform Crime Reports Arrests for Vandalism by Age

Age	Under 10	10–12	13–14	15	16	17	18
Number of Arrests	1,210	7,078	19,215	13,394	15,393	15,212	14,172

Total Number of Arrests: 212,981
Total Arrests under age 18: 71,502

As Table 7-1 shows, the most common age for youths to be arrested for vandalism is between 13–14 years old. As with most crimes, the data also show that as one gets older, the frequency of arrest declines. One of the most common forms of vandalism is graffiti. This term is defined as markings, initials, slogans, or drawings that are written, spray-painted, or sketched on a sidewalk, wall of a building, public restroom, or the like.[24] Graffiti artists, or *taggers,* have been a nuisance problem for officials and community residents for some time, but particularly in the 1980s, when visible representations of gang affiliation became an important part of the physical and social landscapes. Efforts by communities and transportation officials resulted in significant inroads to reducing the evidence of graffiti. However, anecdotal evidence suggests that this form of vandalism has been on the increase all over the country. While no official data is kept on the extent of graffiti, many communities are increasingly finding it a challenge to their quality of life.

Types of Graffiti and Artists

There are three major types of modern graffiti art. The most basic type is a *Tag*, in which the artist writes his name in his own unique style. A more advanced form of tagging is a *Throw-up*, in which the artist may use bubble-letters to create a more intricate design. The next type of graffiti is a *Piece*, which is short for masterpiece, and usually consists of a scene of well-known characters with some sort of slogan. This type of graffiti often requires the collaboration of multiple artists.[25]

Some of the available evidence indicates that approximately half of graffiti artists come from white middle- and upper-class homes, especially concentrated in suburban areas.[26] Though the art form was once originally relegated to low-income urban youths, the popularity of hip-hop as a cultural phenomenon brought graffiti to a wider audience.[27] From a theoretical perspective, one way to explain the popularity of graffiti and its practitioners would be to apply Marx's theory of alienation. In other words, some youths engage in graffiti as a form of political and social expression in an effort to call attention to their current economic and physical plight. Similar to Marx's ideas of the proletariat developing a sense of *class-consciousness*, graffiti serves as a vehicle for youths to reject the existing structure which perpetuates the exploitation of the less powerful classes. Instead of simply being a nameless and faceless part of capitalism, graffiti artists post their names in as many places as possible to let the world know that they still exist.[28] Other artists may turn to graffiti because of boredom, the need for self-expression, or because they hope their work might benefit them economically by being noticed by a potential benefactor. Still others use graffiti as a way to mark certain territory, such as in the case of a gang who wants to identify the boundaries of their turf.[29]

Case Study
Tagging with Baby Z

What do you make of Baby Z's argument that he should not be charged with vandalism? If you were to advocate for him, can you make an argument that what Baby Z did is actually considered a community service and an artistic expression rather than a criminal act?

Broken Windows Theory, The Police, and Graffiti

On one hand, there are those who argue that graffiti should not be considered a crime, as it is little more than artistic expression in public. However, officials note that this activity constitutes the defacement of public and private property that violates legal ordinances. For those police officials who embrace community policing and the broken windows theory, the problems related to graffiti are not the act per se, but the symbolic message its presence conveys. The broken windows philosophy argues that small problems can quickly become bigger ones unless the issue is addressed effectively.[30]

For example, let's suppose that an abandoned warehouse exists in a given community. One day a kid throws a rock through the window of the warehouse, breaking it. If the window is not repaired, soon other kids realize that no one is taking care of the building. Given how much fun it might be to throw rocks through windows, soon many kids are breaking windows at the warehouse.

Then a graffiti artist sees the broken windows and concludes that the abandoned warehouse is a clean canvas on which to display his art. So he tags the building. Other tagger crews then join in and "decorate" the building. This, coupled with the broken windows, creates an image about the building and the area around it. Then let's suppose neighborhood family is moving and do not want to take their old furniture to the landfill (in part because it is far away and also because they may have to pay a fee to dispose of the furniture). They decide to leave it in the parking lot of the warehouse because they think no one will care.

Drug dealers and addicts then begin to use parts of the warehouse because none of the neighbors use the street on which the warehouse is located since they think it is unsafe. Suddenly the area has become crime-ridden and the police are faced with an assortment of problems in that neighborhood. If they only focused on answering the calls for service in that area, the problems would likely get worse. It is only when they take a proactive approach and begin to address the small problems before they become big ones that they can have an impact on the area.

Finally, there is the gang connection to graffiti. Tagger crews are one of the latest groups to receive classification under the gang label. It consists of groups of youths whose reason for existence is graffiti, and each group competes with other crews to see who can put up the most graffiti in a given time period and/or area. What was once a tool by street gangs to stake out their turf, tagging has literally taken on a life of its own. It is now considered sport by a growing proportion of youth from all types of neighborhoods.

For example, some estimates show that there are an estimated 600 active crews in Los Angeles County and approximately 30,000 taggers.[31]

In San Jose, CA, for example, in 2006, the city experienced only 129 incidents of graffiti, however in 2007, that number jumped to 2,594.[32] While this may give the impression that San Jose has a gang problem on its hands, especially since many gang members use graffiti to mark their territory, only about 4% of the graffiti in the United States is gang-related, according to some experts.[33] Still, graffiti contributes to problems in other ways, such as creating a climate of fear due to the disorder it represents.

Case Study
Conclusion: What to Do with Baby Z

While one could technically argue that Baby Z's efforts are artistic in nature and while one might even make the case that he did not intend to commit vandalism, Baby Z did not obtain permission from the owners of the various buildings to spray paint their walls. As a result, Baby Z is guilty of vandalism. In all likelihood, given these circumstances, a judge might not detain Baby Z for his actions; instead he might require him to pay a fine, paint over his artwork, and/or place him on probation for a period of time. At the same time, a judge might also use this as an opportunity to begin a redevelopment of the area in which Baby Z operated. This can be accomplished by appealing to the owners of the buildings, as well as community residents, on ways to improve the aesthetic value of the area and include Baby Z's talents as part of that process. What would you do if you were the judge in this case?

Underage Drinking

When children ask their parents for a sip of wine or beer, they sometimes see it as cute, particularly if the child is a toddler. In older children, parents often use the request to drink as instructional—to teach their children about alcohol. When teens start drinking, parents often use the experience as an opportunity to provide a lesson in judgment, responsibility, and choices. As teens enter college, parents sometimes think that drinking will be a normal part of the college experience. Few parents ever think of these behaviors as necessarily problematic. However, underage drinking is actually one of the most significant social problems of in the United States.

According to the latest figures, specifically the 2009 National Drug Use and Health Survey (NDUHS), about 11 million persons aged 12 to 20 reported drinking alcohol in the past month, which is approximately 27% of this age group. Approximately 7 million were binge drinkers, and 2.3 million were heavy drinkers. The NDUHS defines binge drinking as having five or more drinks on the same occasion: either at the same time or within a couple of hours of each other on at least one day in the past 30 days. Current use is defined as having at least one drink in the past 30 days while heavy drinking consists of someone who has had five or more drinks on the same occasion on each of five or more days in the past 30.

Underage drinkers do not vary much by gender, as indicated by Table 7.2.

Table 7-2[34]
National Drug Use and Health Survey
Alcohol Use by Gender

Type of Alcohol Use	Males	Females
Current Use	29%	25%
Binge Drinking	21%	16%
Heavy Use	7%	4%

The data shows slightly more males than females reported current alcohol use (29% vs. 25%, respectively), whereas males are more likely to engage in binge drinking (21% vs. 16%) and heavy drinking (7% vs. 4%).

Table 7-3[35]
National Drug Use and Health Survey
Alcohol Use by Race/Ethnicity

	Current Use	Binge Drinking
White	31%	22%
African American	21%	9%
Hispanic	25%	18%
Native American	22%	18%
Asian American	16%	7%

With regard to race and ethnicity, as shown in Table 7-3, past month alcohol use rates for underage drinkers was highest among Whites, at almost 31%. About 25% of Hispanics, 22% of Native Americans, 21% of African Americans, and 16% of Asian Americans reported drinking within the past month. Whites were also most likely to report binge drinking (22%), followed by Native Americans and Hispanics (18% each). Asians and African Americans were the least likely to report binge drinking (7% and 9% respectively).[36]

Additionally, there is a connection between underage drinking and drug use. Underage drinkers were three times more likely than persons 21 years or older to use illicit drugs within two hours of alcohol use on their last reported drinking occasion (17.5% vs. 5%). The most commonly reported drug used by underage drinkers in combination with alcohol was marijuana, which was used by 17% of current underage drinkers (1.7 million persons) on their last occurrence.[37]

The data suggest that underage drinking is a serious and significant problem for teens. In fact, in 2007, the Surgeon General called underage drinking an "epidemic" and urged parents to recognize the problem it presents to all Americans. Citing the psychological and physical threats underage drinking presents to society, Kenneth Moritsugu, M.D., M.P.H., the acting Surgeon General, issued a National Call to Action to stop underage drinking and to keep others from starting. He states: "Alcohol remains the most heavily abused substance by America's youth. This Call to Action is attempting to change the culture and attitudes toward drinking in America. We can no longer ignore what alcohol is doing to our children."[38]

Evidence of the significance of underage drinking is also seen in crime statistics. Arrests for liquor law violations are the highest of all categories of status offenses. Moreover, liquor law violations are the most likely of all status offenses to be adjudicated. As noted in Table 7-4, in 2009, the Uniform Crime Reports (UCR) noted 447,496 arrests for liquor law violations, 88,370 of which were those under the age of 18 (see Table 7-4).

The alarming findings by the 2009 Drug Use and Health study are underscored by other surveys on underage drinking. A 2002 study by the National Center on Substance Abuse at Columbia University (CASA), entitled Teen Tipplers: America's Underage Drinking Epidemic, found that alcohol is the biggest drug problem among children and young adults. CASA estimates that the annual costs of alcohol use and abuse are approximately $184.6 billion. Approximately 30% of those costs, nearly $53 billion, are related to underage drinking. The costs are seen in alcohol-related traffic accidents, violent crime, injuries, accidental deaths, suicide attempts, fetal alcohol syndrome, and treatment for alcohol abuse.[40]

Each year, over three million teens between the ages of 12 and 17 take a drink of alcohol for the first time. Despite many programs

Table 7-4[39]
2009 Uniform Crime Reports
Liquor Law Arrests by Age

Age	Arrests
Under 10	101
10–12	622
13–14	7,324
15	13,009
16	24,825
17	42,489
18	74,907
19	82,717
20	67,585

to address the War on Drugs, most high school students are touched by alcohol far more extensively than any other type of drug. By their senior year in high school, nearly 81% of teens have tried alcohol. This figure exceeds the percentage of seniors who have smoked cigarettes (70%) or those who have used marijuana (47%). In contrast, only about 29% of high school seniors have used another illegal drug.[41] Thus, despite the fear associated with drugs like crack, crank, heroin, marijuana, and other illicit drugs, and despite the many efforts to educate youth on the dangers of using them (e.g. D.A.R.E.), alcohol presents the biggest threat to American teens.

Underage drinking is not simply a high school phenomenon. While more teens drink as they get older, many have their first alcoholic drink before age 13, which can lead to an increased risk of developing a problem with alcohol. In other words, age matters: about one in five kids who begin drinking before age 21 report problems with alcohol compared to only about 7% of those who waited until majority age to start drinking. Early drinkers are also more likely to binge drink. One study found that while fewer underage students were using alcohol than in the past, those who did drink tended to do so in excess.[42] In 2002, 21.1% of ninth graders, 32.2% of tenth graders, 34% of eleventh graders and 41.6% of twelfth graders reported binge drinking in the past 30 days. In total, almost a third, more than five million high school students, binge drink.[43]

In 2009, CASA's survey of American Attitudes on Substance Abuse found that two-thirds of all teens who drink on a monthly basis also get drunk at least once in a typical month. Moreover, although the other one-third of teens do not usually drink with the intention to get drunk, they still drink alcohol on a monthly basis. Perhaps most alarming, 8 of 10 seventeen-year-old drinkers get drunk at least once in a typical month.[44]

Early alcohol use may have long-lasting consequences. Young people who begin drinking before the age of 21 are more than twice as likely to develop alcohol-related problems, and individuals who begin drinking before age 15 are four times more likely to become alcohol dependent than those who do not drink before age 21.[45] The real problem with using alcohol at an early age, even if it is to simply experiment, is that most who try it do not stop. One study found that among high school seniors who have tried alcohol— over 90% are still drinking in the twelfth grade. Students who engage in regular alcohol use as teens are at the greatest risk for becoming binge drinkers in college.[46]

Research has shown that students who enter college as non-drinkers will likely remain that way through the first two years of college. High school students who drink alcohol more than 10 times in a month are likely to drink in their freshman year of college.[47] Preventing student alcohol use and abuse during the early teen years may prove to be the most effective way of reducing the high rates of alcohol use and binge drinking in college. What is not clear, however, is whether starting to drink at an early age actually causes alcoholism or whether it simply indicates an existing vulnerability to alcohol use disorders.[48] Some evidence indicates that genetic factors may contribute to the relationship between early drinking and subsequent alcoholism.[49]

The Role of the Media
in Underage Drinking

Another report by CASA revealed that underage drinkers consume about 20% of all alcohol consumed in the United States, spending $22.5 billion of the $116.2 billion spent on beer, wine, and liquor.[50] The major portion of the alcohol consumed by underage drinkers is beer. CASA estimates that $17.2 billion was attributable to beer, $4.3 billion to distilled spirits and $1 billion to wine.[51] Clearly underage drinkers represent a significant portion of the alcohol industry's customer base.

Consequently, the alcohol industry spends billions of dollars each year on advertising, which includes sponsorship of events, Internet advertising, and product placements in movies and TV shows.[52] Image advertising, which markets a persona or an image rather than the quality of a product, is aggressively used by the alcohol industry. Several studies suggest that animation and rock music commonly used in beer advertising campaigns have wide appeal among children and young teens. Children are more familiar with the Budweiser characters in commercials than with virtually any other animated figure. The implication of this is that the more they identify with the character, the more likely they will choose to drink.[53]

In a series of studies in New Zealand, researchers found that positive attitudes about alcohol advertisements were related to increased adolescent drinking and intentions to drink. In addition, adolescent males who could remember alcohol advertisements at age 15 consumed more alcohol at age 18.[54] What is particularly compelling about this body of work is that alcohol advertising in New Zealand is subject to much more stringent regulations than in the U.S., yet the relationship between advertising and intentions to drink remains significant.[55]

Experts tend to agree that advertising exerts an influence on teen drinking patterns, but more research is needed to determine the precise relationship between alcohol advertising and underage drinking. The need for such research is particularly important if one considers that beer, the most extensively advertised alcoholic beverage, is also the least expensive, the most widely available, and the top choice of underage drinkers.[56]

Relatively recent additions to the product line of the alcohol beverage industry are a new group of sweet-tasting alcoholic beverages, known as "malternatives" or "alcopops" (e.g., Mike's Hard Lemonade, Smirnoff Ice,). These beverages are sweet, fruit-flavored, malt-based drinks that come in colorful packaging. Most alcopop beverages have approximately five to seven percent alcohol by volume, a level that is comparable to beer.[57]

Given the significance of advertising and its important role in underage drinking, consumer, parent, religious, health, and prevention organizations have stepped up efforts in the past 20 years to reform the advertising of alcoholic beverages. Such efforts resulted in Congressional hearings, government policy statements, and some efforts by the alcohol, advertising, and broadcast industries to promote responsible drinking through public service announcements and other program activities.[58]

Positive images of alcohol use are not just projected by alcohol advertisers; there also is a significant presence of alcohol messages in movies and on primetime television shows.[59] An analysis of 81 G-rated animated films found that nearly half showed characters using or abusing alcohol or tobacco, but a significant proportion do not portray the long-term consequences of tobacco and alcohol use. In 34% of the movies, alcohol use was associated with wealth or luxury. In 19%, alcohol use was associated with sexual activity. Alcohol use on television shows often is depicted without adverse consequences or in association with humor, wealth, status, and professionalism.[60]

Clearly the role of the media is an important consideration in the incidence of underage drinking. As more advertisers target youth as potential customers, even though it would be illegal for them to consume their products, the end result will likely be an increase in underage drinking.

The Impact of Underage Alcohol Use

What are the implications of alcohol use, particularly for teens? There are a host of physical and emotional issues associated with underage drinking. For instance, according to the National Center for Health Statistics National Center for Health Statistics, alcohol is related to the three leading causes of death among teens ages 12 to 18: accidents (including motor vehicle traffic fatalities and drowning), homicide, and suicide. Underage drinking is associated with teen pregnancy and has also been linked to poor educational achievement, delinquency, and drug abuse.

Academic Achievement

Students who abuse alcohol are less likely to do well in school and to show a commitment to schooling. Heavy and binge drinkers between the ages of 12 and 17 have been found to be far more likely than nondrinkers to say that their school work is poor, and four to five times more likely to say that they cut classes or skip school. Students at high risk for alcohol abuse also are at risk for repeating a grade and being absent or suspended from school. High school students who use alcohol or other substances are five times more likely to drop out of school than nonusers.[61]

Physical Health Issues

Young drinkers run the risk of developing numerous health problems due to alcohol use, such as coronary heart disease, stroke, liver cirrhosis, and various forms of cancer. Alcohol abuse is also related to bulimia and anorexia nervosa, as well as with depression and anxiety disorders, particularly among girls. Research suggests that approximately 23% percent of women with bulimia and 6% of those with anorexia have alcohol abuse and/or dependence.

Sexual Behavior

Alcohol use is also closely related to teen sexual activity. Teens who drink are more likely than teens who do not drink to have sex, to have sexual intercourse at an earlier age, and to have more partners. About 5.6 million 15- to 24-year-olds report having unprotected sex because they were drinking or using drugs at the time. Perhaps more importantly, while the majority of high-school-age drinkers and drug users report using condoms, there still exists a large percentage of teens who are at risk for HIV, other sexually transmitted diseases, and pregnancy. One study found that 49% of sexually active teens said they were more likely to have sex if they had been drinking and 17% of the sexually active teens said that they were less likely to use a condom when they had been drinking.[62]

Psychological Effects

The available research indicates that approximately 35% of individuals with a mood disorder and almost half of those with anxiety disorders are alcohol dependent. What is not clear is the causal order of these two problems. In some cases, mental disorders occurred after the discovery of alcohol abuse while in other cases, it was a consequence of the disorder.[63]

Suicide is also a problem for teen drinkers. While suicide is the third leading cause of death for young people ages 15 to 24 years old, alcohol use is a significant risk factor for suicide attempts. Alcohol is estimated to be involved in about 10% of teen suicides. In one study of suicide among adolescents, 70% of young people who attempted suicide frequently used alcohol and/or other drugs.[64]

Additionally, adolescent heavy drinkers and binge drinkers are more than twice as likely as nondrinkers to say they contemplate suicide.[65] The estimated national cost of alcohol-related adolescent suicide is $1.5 billion annually. Alcohol may be related to suicide in several ways. For example, drinking may reduce inhibitions and impair the judgment of someone who is contemplating suicide, making suicide attempts more likely.[66]

Auto Accidents

Alcohol-related motor vehicle fatality rates are nearly twice as high for those between the ages of 18 to 20 compared to those over age 21. In an effort to reduce traffic fatalities associated with alcohol consumption, the National Minimum Drinking Age Act of 1984 required all states to raise the age at which individuals can purchase and publicly possess alcohol to 21. Failure to comply with the act resulted in states losing federal highway funds under the Federal Highway Aid Act. By 1987, all states had complied with the 21 minimum drinking age law.[67]

In 2009, about a third of students reported riding in a car at least once during the past 30 days with a driver who had been drinking, and 13% of students reported that they had driven a vehicle at least once while under the influence of alcohol.[68] Male students are twice as likely as female students to have driven after drinking alcohol. About 16% of binge drinkers and about a third of heavy drinkers said that they drive while under the influence. Another study of young drivers found that only 15% of those surveyed reported using a sober designated driver when drinking.[69]

The minimum drinking age law, the influence of such groups as Mothers Against Drunk Driving (MADD) and Students Against Drunk Driving (SADD), as well as a reduction of the legal blood alcohol limit (BAC) for driving while intoxicated from 0.10 to 0.08 have been part of the explanation for the reduction of traffic fatalities. However, the fact that a third of students are in vehicles with someone drinking suggests that there is still work to be done with regard to changing attitudes about driving while impaired. While there is room for optimism, the fact that nearly one in five students drove at some point while intoxicated suggests more needs to be done to curb underage drinking.

Underage Smoking

Although it is considered a status offense, and even though it is not noted in the Uniform Crime Reports or the Juvenile Court Statistics Juvenile Court Statistics, teen smoking is considered a serious social problem in the United States. In fact, it is considered one of the most preventable of all diseases and affects millions of teenagers each year. The use of tobacco products, which includes cigarettes, cigars, and forms of smokeless tobacco products, such as "chew" and "snuff," cause a host of problems for parents, teens, and the general public. In fact, the use of tobacco, specifically smoking, has links to alcohol abuse and other forms of illicit drug abuse.

Extent of the Problem

Perhaps the two most comprehensive measures of teen smoking come from the National Drug Use and Health Survey (NDUHS) and the Monitoring the Future Study (MFS). According to the MFS, the statistics for the use of cigarettes and alcohol, considered licit drugs, are alarming.

According to the survey, nearly half of American youth have tried cigarettes by the 12th grade and nearly a quarter of 12th graders are current smokers. An equal number of 8th graders have tried cigarettes and about 10% are considered current smokers. While some experts expressed a level of optimism concerning the decline in cigarette use in the 1990s, by 2006, rates were higher than before the decline. This is true not only of the use of cigarettes but also attitudes about them. Many changes about cigarettes and smoking in the early 1990s were attributed to the reduction in cigarette advertising as well as anti-smoking campaigns funded by tobacco companies as part of their overall legal settlement. Further, the cost of cigarettes, which rose substantially during this period, was also seen as a deterrent among teens (these costs were designed in part to offset the expenses associated with the tobacco settlement as well as a source of revenue for states in the form of increased excise taxes).[70]

Another area of concern is smokeless tobacco, which comes in two forms. "Snuff Snuff" is finely ground tobacco usually sold in tins, either loose or in packets. It is held in the mouth between the lip or cheek and the gums. "Chew Chew" is a leafy form of tobacco, usually sold in pouches. It is held in the mouth and can be chewed.

Smokeless tobacco is also sometimes called "spit" tobacco because users spit out the tobacco juices and saliva stimulated by the tobacco that accumulates in the mouth.[71] While this represents a much smaller segment of the tobacco-using teen population, the changes in use, disapproval, and availability are similar to cigarettes.[72]

According to NDUHS, in 2009 an estimated 70 million Americans aged 12 or older were current users (as defined as using within the past thirty days) of a tobacco product. This represents about 28% of the population in that age category. Among underage smokers, those between the ages of 12 and 17, there were 3.3 million users of tobacco products in 2009, of which 2.7 million used cigarettes. In 2009, 2.4% of 12- to 13-year-olds, 9.2% of 14- to 15-year-olds, and 20.6% of 16- to 17-year-olds were current cigarette smokers.[73] Clearly cigarettes are the preferred tobacco product among underage youth. Smokeless tobacco rates were only about 2% for the 12–17 age group.[74] Males and females are about equally likely to use cigarettes in this age group (9.3% vs. 8.6%).[75]

With regard to race and ethnicity, as Table 7-5 shows, among youths aged 12 to 17, cigarette smoking was more common among Whites than African Americans (10.6% vs. 5.1%), while about 8% of Hispanics and nearly 12% of Native Americans, along with 2.5% of Asians, reported using a tobacco product within the last month.[76]

Table 7-5[77]
National Drug Use and Health Survey
Youths 12 to 17 Years of Age
Past 30 Day Tobacco Use by Ethnicity

Race/Ethnicity	Percentage
Whites	10.6%
African Americans	5.1%
Hispanic/Latino	7.5%
Asian American	2.5%
Hawaiian/Pacific Islander	11.6%

The Connection of Tobacco Use and Other Drugs

According to the National Drug Use and Health Survey (2009) (the Monitoring the Future (2009) and the latest CASA (2009) reports), the use of illicit drugs and alcohol was more common among current cigarette smokers than non-smokers. That is, people who smoke tend also to take other drugs, rendering cigarette smoking a gateway activity to different forms of drug abuse. In fact, cigarette smokers are five times more likely to use illicit drugs compared to non-smokers (20.2% vs. 4.1%). Alcohol abuse is also more common among smokers compared to non-smokers. Alcohol use was reported by over two-thirds of current cigarette smokers compared with less than half by those who did not smoke cigarettes (67.6% vs. 46.6%). This connection also relates to binge drinking, where cigarette smokers are approximately three times more likely to binge drink than non-smokers (43.8% vs. 15.7%). Heavy drinking is most noted among smokers, who are five times more likely to be heavy drinkers than those who do not smoke (16.1% vs. 3.5%).

It also seems that cigarette smoking is connected to using other tobacco products as well. While only about 5% of cigarette smokers used smokeless tobacco, they are still twice as likely to use smokeless tobacco than non-smokers (5% vs. 2.6%). Additionally, cigarette smokers were about four times more likely to smoke cigars than those who did not smoke cigarettes (12.6% vs. 3.3%). Clearly the addictive properties associated with smoking cigarettes make it much more likely for a user to resort to other forms of tobacco as well.[78]

Obviously the real problems associated with cigarettes come when they are smoked. Tobacco smoke contains thousands of different chemicals which are released into the air as particles and gases. Many toxins are present in high concentrations and nearly 60 of the chemicals emitted have been shown to cause cancer.[79]

In the 1950s tar in tobacco smoke was discovered to be associated with the increased risk of lung cancer. In response, tobacco companies gradually reduced the tar levels in cigarettes. Although there is a small decrease in the risk of lung cancer by using lower tar cigarettes, research suggests that these benefits are negated by the tendency of smokers to smoke more of them or to inhale more deeply. Also, a study by the American Cancer Society American Cancer Society found that the use of filtered, lower tar cigarettes may be the cause of adenocarcinoma, a particular kind of lung cancer.[80]

"Nicotine," an alkaloid, is an extremely powerful drug. Nicotine is contained in the moisture of the tobacco leaf: when the cigarette is lit, it evaporates, attaching itself to the tobacco smoke inhaled by the smoker. It is absorbed by the body very quickly, reaching the brain within seconds. It stimulates the central nervous system, increasing the heart beat rate and blood pressure, leading to the heart needing more oxygen. "Carbon monoxide," the main poisonous gas in car exhausts, is present in all cigarette smoke. It binds to hemoglobin much more readily than oxygen, thus causing the blood to carry less oxygen. Heavy smokers may have the oxygen-carrying power of their blood cut by as much as 15%.[81]

The Effects of Smoking

Cigarette smoking during childhood and adolescence produces significant health problems among young people, including an increase in the number and severity of respiratory illnesses, decreased physical fitness, and potential reduction in the rate of lung growth and the level of maximum lung functioning. An estimated 440,000 Americans die each year from diseases caused by smoking.[82]

Each day, nearly 6,000 children under 18 years of age start smoking; of these, nearly 2,000 will become regular smokers. That is almost 800,000 annually. Approximately 90% of smokers begin smoking before the age of 21. Adolescents who smoke regularly can have just as hard a time quitting as long-time smokers. Of adolescents who have smoked at least 100 cigarettes in their lifetime, most of them report that they would like to quit, but are not able to do so.[83]

According to the MFS study, the greatest preventable cause of disease and mortality in the United States is cigarette smoking. According to the American Heart Association, repeated warnings have alerted us to the risks of lung cancer and heart disease associated with smoking and exposure to secondhand tobacco smoke.

Some argue that heavy use of cigarette smoking is problematic but those who only smoke occasionally do not pose as high a risk as heavy smokers. However, in a study published in a 2006 issue of the *Journal of Epidemiology and Public Health,* Danish researchers found that smoking as few as three to five cigarettes per day substantially increased the risk of heart attack and death. This finding was true for both men and women, but was especially true in women, in whom "light" smoking (those who smoke only a few cigarettes a day) resulted in a 50% higher incidence of both heart attack and death as compared to men.[84]

Previous studies on light smokers also showed that smoking a relatively small number of cigarettes daily was hazardous to one's health, but in these studies a cutoff of 10 to 20 cigarettes per day was used. Mei-Chen, Davies, and Kandel's (2006) study was the first to document that even a very small number of cigarettes per day is a problem. This new study was accomplished by analyzing data from the Copenhagen City Heart Study, in which 14,223 individuals without evidence of heart disease were followed from 1976 to 1998. A relatively large proportion of these people turned out to be smokers. The researchers found that the more cigarettes one smokes per day, the higher the risk. But the risk remains substantial all the way down to three cigarettes per day. What this means is that cigarette smokers who convince themselves that "cutting back" is good enough are actually still vulnerable.

Effects of Secondhand Smoke

Secondhand smoke is a byproduct of cigarette, cigar, or pipe smoking. Secondhand smoke occurs when tobacco burns or when smokers exhale, and it is inhaled involuntarily by nonsmokers. Secondhand smoke is composed of two types of smoke. The first is called *side stream smoke,* which is the smoke released from the burning end of a cigarette, a cigar, or from tobacco burning in the bowl of a pipe. The second is called *mainstream smoke,* which is exhaled by a smoker. When nonsmokers are exposed to secondhand smoke, they inhale many of the same cancer-causing chemicals that smokers inhale. According to the U.S. Surgeon General, cigarette smoke contains more than 4,000 chemical compounds, including more than 50 cancer-causing chemicals, and at least 250 chemicals that are either toxic or carcinogenic.[85]

Both side stream and mainstream smoke are dangerous to nonsmokers. For example, because side stream smoke is generated at lower temperatures and under different conditions than mainstream smoke, it contains higher concentrations of many of the toxins found in cigarettes. The U.S. Environmental Protection Agency, the National Toxicology Program, and the International Agency have designated secondhand smoke as a known human carcinogen for Research on Cancer. The National Institute also lists secondhand smoke as an occupational carcinogen for Occupational Safety and Health.[86]

Former U.S. Surgeon General Richard H. Carmona issued a warning about the dangers of secondhand smoke. In the report, *The Health Consequences of Involuntary Exposure to Tobacco Smoke,* Carmona said there is no risk-free level of exposure to secondhand smoke. His report shows that nonsmokers who are exposed to secondhand smoke increase their risk of developing heart disease by 25% to 30% and their risk of lung cancer by 20% to 30%. This is a major public health concern, because nearly half of all nonsmoking Americans are regularly exposed to secondhand smoke. The Surgeon General's report shows that secondhand smoke exposure can cause heart disease and lung cancer in nonsmoking adults and is a known cause of sudden infant death syndrome (SIDS), respiratory problems, ear infections, and asthma attacks in infants and children.

The report shows that even brief exposure to secondhand smoke can cause immediate harm. The only way to protect nonsmokers from the dangerous chemicals in secondhand smoke is to eliminate smoking indoors, because even the most sophisticated ventilation systems cannot completely eliminate secondhand smoke exposure and only smoke-free environments afford full protection.

Many U.S. cities and businesses have banned indoor smoking recently, but others have resisted for fear of losing regular customers or appearing to discriminate against smokers.[87]

Have Media Campaigns Reduced Teen Smoking?

As was mentioned, the rates of tobacco products are increasing despite anti-smoking campaigns, cost increases, and the tobacco industry's proposed lack of ad campaigns targeting teens. But questions remain about whether the industry has been honest about their efforts to reduce teen smoking. While tobacco-makers emphatically deny that they target young people, many of their promotions just happen to appeal to the underage smokers on whom they depend for future business. These efforts seem to be pitched at three levels. First, like the alcohol industry, tobacco manufacturers have begun marketing flavored cigarettes with names such as Kauai Kolada, Twista Lime, and Mandarin Mint, giving curious teens new reasons to try smoking. R.J. Reynolds, which markets the Camel "exotic blends," says they are not aimed at teens. Yet, according to surveys released in May 2004 by the Roswell Park Cancer Institute in Buffalo, about 20% of smokers ages 17 through 19 tried a flavored cigarette, compared with less than 9% of smokers older than 19. At age 55, the interest in flavored products dropped to 2%.[88]

Second, also like their alcohol counterparts, the tobacco industry seems to have increased its spending on promotions despite agreeing to curtail or stop certain types of marketing. According to a Federal Trade Commission report in 2003, since signing a deal in 1998 with state officials across the country to curtail certain types of marketing, the industry has more than doubled its expenditures on advertising and promotions. In 2003, major tobacco companies spent $15.1 billion on marketing strategies — $22 for every dollar the states spent on tobacco prevention. The bulk of industry spending was on price discounts.[89]

Summary

While chronic non-violent offenders tend not to gain as much national attention for their activities, this chapter has shown that the nature of their activities is problematic and requires a considerable amount of resources and attention. Whether it is the financial burden created by computer hackers, or the economic costs to remove the artistic expressions on public buildings by graffiti artists, or the physical and health risks associated with underage drinking and smoking, these activities can have a considerable impact on society. From the available evidence, it would also appear that non-violent chronic offenders can generate a considerable level of fear and concern over victimization: the fears stemming from identity theft and other forms of hacking have created a multi-billion-dollar a year industry, while the fear generated from the disorder often associated with graffiti can have a significant impact on the quality of life and crime levels in a given neighborhood. In sum, an argument could be made that this group of offenders, largely due to their size and the short- and long-term impact of their activities, represents a significant portion of the delinquency problem.

Notes

1. Yar, M. 2005. "Computer Hacking: Just Another Case of Juvenile Delinquency?" *The Howard Journal of Criminal Justice*, 44(4): 387–399.

2. Ethical Hacking: Student courseware. Ec-Council. www.ec-council.org Goodwin, B. (2004, March 16). "Hacking course offers insights into the mind and method of bad guys." *Computer Weekly*.

3. Yar, 2005.

4. Ibid.

5. See Taylor, R. W. 2000. "Hacker, Phone Phreakers and Virus Makers." In C.R. Swanson, Chamelin, N. C,. and Territo, L. *Criminal Investigation*, 7th edition. New York: McGraw-Hill.

6. See for instance, Kremen, S. 2008. Computer Forensics Online. Available at http://www.shk-dplc.com/cfo/articles/hack.htm.

7. Ibid.

8. Schmalleger, F. 2007. *Criminology Today* 4th Edition. Upper Saddle River, NJ: Prentice-Hall.

9. Barlow, J. P. 1990. "Crime and Puzzlement: In Advance of the Law on the Electronic Frontier." *Whole Earth Review,* Fall, 44.

10. Adapted from Maxfield, J. 1985. *Computer Bulletin Boards and the Hacker Problem." EDPACS, the Electronic Data Processing Audit, Control and Security Newsletter.* Arlington, VA: Automation Training Center.

11. Selwyn, N. 2003. "Doing IT for the Kids: Re-Examining Children, Computers and the Information Society." *Media, Culture & Society*, 15(3): 351–378.

12. See http://www.kevinmitnick.com/press.php.

13. Kremen 2008.

14. Ibid.

15. See http://www.kevinmitnick.com/press.php.

16. Selwyn, 2003.

17. Sandell, C. 2009. "President Obama says the nation's digital security is a top priority for his administration." *ABC News,* May 29th http://abclocal.go.com/kfsn/story?section=news/politics&id=6839437.

18. Yurcik, B. S., Doss, D. 2001. *Ethical Hacking: The Security Justification. Ethics of Electronic Information in the 21st Century Symposium.* University of Memphis: Memphis TN. See also McGee, M. K. 2005. "Hacker Boot Camp Helps Good Guys Outsmart Internet Troublemakers." Retrieved from http://www.informationweek.com. See also Sanders, A. D. 2003. "Utilizing simple hacking techniques to teach system security and hacker identification." *Journal of Information Systems Education*, 14(1), 5.

19. Leung, L. 2005. "Hackers for Hire: Bringing in Ethical Hacker Consultants is the Latest in Security Defense. http://www.networkworld.com. See also Logan, P. Y. 2002. "Crafting an undergraduate information security emphasis within information technology." *Journal of Information Systems Education*, 13(3): 177–182.

20. Ibid.

21. Carnevale, D. 2005. "Basic training for anti-hackers: An intensive summer program drills students on cyber security skills." *Chronicle of Higher Education,* 52(5): 41–41.

22. http://dictionary.reference.com/browse/vandalism.

23. U.S. Department of Justice, Federal Bureau of Investigation. 2009. *Crime in the United States.* Table 38. Available at http://www2.fbi.gov/ucr/cius2009/data/table_38.html.

24. Ferrell, J. 1993. *Crimes of Style: Urban Graffiti and the Politics of Criminality.* New York: Garland.

25. Walsh, M. 1996. *Graffito.* Berkley, California: North Atlantic Books. See also Reed, A. W. 1977.*Classic American Graffiti: Lexical Evidence from Folk Epigraphy in Western North America.* Waukesha, WI: Maledicta Press, 1977.

26. See for instance Wimsatt, W. U. 1994. *Bomb the Suburbs: Graffiti, Freight-hopping, Race and the Search for Hip-Hop's Moral Center.* Chicago: The Subway and Elevated Press.

27. Stocker, D. 1971. "Social Analysis of Graffiti." *Journal of American Folklore,* 85: 358.

28. Powers, L. A. 1999. "Whatever Happened to the Graffiti Art Movement?" *Journal of Popular Culture,* 29 (4): 137–142.

29. Ibid.

30. Wilson, J. Q. and Kelling, G. 1982. "Broken Windows: The Police and Neighborhood Safety." *Atlantic Monthly, available at http://www.theatlantic.com/magazine/archive/1982/03/broken-windows/4465/*

31. Wooten and Blazak 2000.

32. Kimbrel, J. 2008. City Tags Graffiti Problem." *Spartan Daily,* February 26th. Available at http://media.www.thespartandaily.com/media/storage/paper852/news/2008/02/26/News/City-Tags.Graffiti.Problem-3234554.shtml accessed July 22, 2008.

33. Recycling and Waste Commission of Santa Clara County, CA. 2008. *Graffiti Q and A.* http://www.sccgov.org/portal/site/iwm/agencyarticle?path=%2Fv7%2FIntegrated%20Waste%20Management%20(DIV)%2FLitter%20and%20%20Graffiti&contentId=d28bdc18dfb34010VgnVCMP230004adc4a92____ accessed July 22, 2008.

34. Department of Health and Human Services, Office of Applied Studies. 2009. *National Drug Abuse and Health Survey.* Washington, DC: U.S. Government Printing Office. Available at http://oas.samhsa.gov/NSDUH/2k9NSDUH/2k9ResultsP.pdf.

35. Ibid.

36. Ibid.

37. Ibid.

38. Ibid.

39. Department of Justice, *Crime in the United States,* 2009.

40. The National Center on Addiction and Substance Abuse (CASA) at Columbia University. 2002. *The economic value of underage drinking and adult excessive drinking to the alcohol industry.* New York: National Center on Addiction and Substance.

41. Ibid.

42. Wechsler, H., Kuo, M., Lee, H., & Dowdall, G. W. 2000. "Environmental Correlates of Underage Alcohol Use and Related Problems of College Students." *American Journal of Preventive Medicine,* 19(1): 24–29.

43. CASA, 2002.

44. CASA, 2009. *National Survey of American Attitudes on Substance Abuse XIV: Teens and Parents.* Available at http://www.casacolumbia.org/articletfiles/380-2009%20Teen%20Survey%20Report%20.pdf.

45. CASA, 2002.

46. Wechsler et al., 2000.

47. Kluger, J. 2001. "How to Manage Teen Drinking (the smart way)." *Time,* 157: 42–44.

48. Dawson, D. A. 2000. "The Link Between Family History and Early Onset Alcoholism: Earlier Initiation of Drinking or More Rapid Development of Dependence?" Journal of studies on Alcoholism 61(5): 637–646.

49. Brown, S. A. and D'Amico, E. J. 2001. "Outcomes of Alcohol Treatment for Adolescents" in Galanter, M. (ed.) *Research Developments in Alcoholism, Vol. 15: Services Research in the Era of Managed Care.* New York Kluer Academic/Plenum, 307–327. See also Deas, D., and Thomas, S.E. 2002. "Comorbid Psychiatric Factors Contributing to Adolescent Alcohol and Other Drug Use." Alcohol Research & Health 26(2): 116–121.

50. Centers for Disease Control and Prevention. 2000. *Fact sheet: Youth Risk Behavior Trends from CDC's 1991, 1993, 1995, 1997, and 1999 Youth Risk Behavior Surveys.* Atlanta, GA: U.S. Department of Health and Human Services, Centers for Disease Control and Prevention. Centers for Disease Control and Prevention. 2000. "Youth Risk Behavior Surveillance, United States, 1999." *Morbidity and Mortality Weekly Report* (MMWR), 49(SS05).

51. CASA, 2002.

52. Scheir, L. M., Botvin, G. J., Griffin, K. W., & Diaz, T. 2000. "Dynamic Growth Modelsof Self-Esteem and Adolescent Alcohol Use." *Journal of Early Adolescence,* 20(2): 178–209.

53. Hill, S. Y., Shen, S., Lowers, L., & Locke, J. 2000. "Factors Predicting the Onset of Adolescent Drinking in Families at High Risk for Developing Alcoholism." *Biological Psychiatry,* 48(4): 265–275.

54. Johnson, H. L., & Johnson, P. B. 1997. "Understanding Early Adolescent Smoking and Drinking," In B. Bain, H. Janzen, J. Paterson, L. Stewin, & A. Yu (eds*.),psychology and education in the 21st century—Proceedings of the International Council of Psychologists Convention,* 153–158. Edmonton, Alberta: IC Press.

55. See Richter, L., & Richter, D. M. 2001. "Exposure to Parental Tobacco and Alcohol use: Effects on Children's Health and Development. *American Journal of Orthopsychiatry,* 71(2): 182–203.

56. Ibid.

57. Alcohol Foundation. 2001. *"Alcopops* Alcopops" and Kids. Chapel Hill, NC: Alcohol Foundation. See also Merikangas, K. R., Stolar, M., Stevens, D. E., Goulet, J., Preisig, M. A., Fenton, B. 1998. "Familial Transmission of Substance Use Disorders." *Archives of General Psychiatry,* 55(11): 973–979.

58. Biederman, J., Faraone, S. V., Monuteaux, M. C., & Feighner, J. A. 2000. "Patterns of Alcohol and Drug Use in Adolescents can be Predicted by Parental Substance use Disorders. *Pediatrics,* 106(4): 792–797.

59. CASA, 2002.

60. Fletcher, A. C., & Jeffries, B. C. 1999. "Parental Mediators of Associations Between Perceived Authoritative Parenting and Early Adolescent Substance Use." *Journal of Early Adolescence,* 19(4): 465–487.

61. Greenblatt, J. C. 2000. *Patterns of Alcohol Use among Adolescents and Associations with Emotional and Behavioral Problems.* Rockville, MD: Substance Abuse and Mental Health Services Administration.
62. CASA, 2002.
63. National Institute on Alcohol Abuse and Alcoholism. 2000. *10th special report to Congress on Alcohol and Health: Highlights from Current Research.* Rockville, MD: U.S. Department of Health and Human Services.
64. Ibid.
65. Pacific Institute for Research and Evaluation. 2003. *Alcohol Beverage Control Enforcement: A Legal Research Report.* Calverton, MD: Pacific Institute for Research and Evaluation.
66. Greenblatt, 2000.
67. National Highway Traffic Safety Administration. 2002. *Traffic Safety Facts 2000: Alcohol.* Washington, DC: U.S. Department of Transportation.
68. Department of Health and Human Services, Office of Applied Studies. 2009. *National Drug Abuse and Health Survey.* Washington, DC: U.S. Government Printing Office. Available at http://oas.samhsa.gov/NSDUH/2k9NSDUH/2k9ResultsP.pdf.
69. Greenblatt, 2000; National Highway Traffic Safety Administration, 2002.
70. Department of Health and Human Services, Office of Applied Studies. 2009.
71. (MFS 2006).
72. Department of Health and Human Services, Office of Applied Studies. 2009.
73. Ibid.
74. Ibid.
75. Ibid.
76. Ibid.
77. Department of Health and Human Services, Office of Applied Studies. 2009. *National Drug Abuse and Health Survey.*
78. National Institute on Drug Abuse. *Monitoring the Future 2009.* Ann Arbor, MI: University of Michigan.
79. Action on Smoking and Health. Fact Sheet #12. November 2006.

80. American Cancer Society. 2006. Cigarette Smoking Statistics. Available at http://www.americanheart.org/presenter.jhtml?identifier=4559.

81. Action on Smoking and Health, 2006.

82. American Heart Association 2006.

83. Ibid.

84. Mei-Chen H., Davies, M. and Kandel, D. B. 2006. "Epidemiology and Correlates of Daily Smoking and Nicotine Dependence Among Young Adults in the United States, *"American Journal of Public Health* 96(2): 299–308.

85. U.S. Surgeon General's Office 2004. *The Health Consequences of Involuntary Exposure to Tobacco Smoke.* Washington, DC: U.S. Government Printing Office.

86. Ibid.

87. Ibid.

88. Ibid.

89. Federal Trade Commission. 2003. *Cigarette Report.* Available at http://www.ftc.gov/reports/cigarette05/050809cigrpt.pdf.

Index

Note: *f* denotes figure; *t*, table.